Rebooting Local Economies

Rebooting Local Economies

How to Build Prosperous Communities

Robert H. Pittman, Rhonda Phillips, and Amanda Sutt

BUSINESS EXPERT PRESS

Leader in applied, concise business books

Rebooting Local Economies: How to Build Prosperous Communities

First published in 2022 by
Business Expert Press, LLC
222 East 46th Street, New York, NY 10017
www.businessexpertpress.com

ISBN-13: 978-1-63742-254-0 (paperback)
ISBN-13: 978-1-63742-255-7 (e-book)

Business Expert Press Economics and Public Policy Collection

First edition: 2022

10 9 8 7 6 5 4 3 2 1

Description

Why do some communities thrive and grow while others struggle and decline? Smart communities know how to attract and nurture the kinds of businesses and organizations they want to create a vibrant economy and higher quality of life.

The more that elected officials and all residents know about community and economic development, the more the community will prosper. *How to Build Prosperous Communities* **is a practical guide to help communities reach their goals for prosperity.** Numerous examples throughout the book show how communities and regions of all sizes have attained and maintained prosperity in a constantly changing environment.

The book is based on the authors' years of experience helping communities and regions across the country and around the world create their roadmaps to prosperity with better jobs, improved public services, and enhanced amenities.

Keywords

economic development; community development; city growth; prosperous community; rebooting economy; new normal; job creation; city planning; community marketing; community strategic planning; community visioning; community assessment; business attraction; high quality of life; high standard of living

Contents

Testimonials

Rebooting Local Economies: How to Build Prosperous Communities is **highly recommended** by practitioners, elected officials, and others involved in community and economic development.......

"Using real-world examples blended with just the right amount of academic research, Rebooting Local Economies *is the equivalent of a master class in how to build a prosperous community. If you are an economic developer of an American community in need of a turnaround at any level, Robert Pittman, Rhonda Phillips and Amanda Sutt have done the homework for you and produced a blueprint for success. They have distilled the work of community development and improvement to its essence, and they have documented the results that inevitably follow when this recipe is followed. **I encourage every elected community official, city manager and economic developer in the U.S. to read this manual. It's the best book on this topic I have read in a very long time.**"*—**Ron Starner, Executive Vice President, Site Selection Magazine and Conway, Inc., Atlanta, Georgia**

"Rebooting Local Economies: How to Build Prosperous Communities provides real life stories that can put you on a path to building a more prosperous community. If you're an elected official, board member, community volunteer or citizen who aspires to live in a prosperous community, **Rebooting Local Economies: How to Build Prosperous Communities** *is a must read."*—**Glenn McCullough, Jr., Former Mayor, Tupelo, Mississippi, Chairman—Tennessee Valley Authority '01–'05, Executive Director Mississippi Development Authority '15–'20**

*"**You have done almost an impossible task of creating a really concise guide for community development. The case studies are particularly interesting—and compelling.** Strategic planning has long been associated with successful organizations; much time and energy have been devoted to creating plans that, for one reason or another, fail to be implemented.*

In **How to Build Prosperous Communities,** *community leaders are offered a roadmap to community prosperity that can be achieved by breaking the process into manageable components.* The incorporation of important topics for consideration, including impacts from the global health pandemic, as well as contemporary case studies of communities with diverse populations, will provide individuals a masterful approach to changing the culture of their communities in dramatic fashion."—**James F. Mellichamp, President, Piedmont University, Demorest, Georgia**

"The book was very informative—it is a must read for local leadership and a blueprint for success in economic development."—**Greg James, Chair, Board of Commissioners, Rabun County, Georgia**

"The authors do an excellent job outlining economic development initiatives and follow it up with case studies and examples where the initiatives have worked. This quick read is a great tool to have at your fingertips as a City official."—**Chuck Warbington, City Manager, Lawrenceville, Georgia**

"This is a great resource for community leaders to share so they are all working from the same play book for the critical work of community economic development. It is a quick read with easy-to-use resources no matter what level of experience you have."—**Nicole Love Hendrickson, Chairwoman, Board of Commissioners, Gwinnett County, Georgia**

"I have been lucky enough to be part of a team of elected officials that have revitalized our downtown to become the pinnacle example of how to revitalize a city. After reading Rebooting Local Economies, I realize I have not considered many gaps in our economic development plan. **This book gives recent and relevant research to show trends as well as being written for anyone to easily follow regardless if you are in industry or not.** It has left me with many ideas to research and implement that I hadn't considered before. I really enjoyed the read!"—**Greg Whitlock, City Council, Duluth, Georgia**

Preface

Movies about space exploration often show humankind at our best—smart, daring and above all, working together. *The Right Stuff* and *First Man,* respectively, tell the success stories of achieving earth orbit and landing on the moon. *Apollo 13*, on the other hand, begins as a story about failure but ends as a testimony to how people at all levels and pay grades came together to avert disaster and save three brave astronauts. These movies show that while the astronauts obviously must be well-trained and knowledgeable, the support teams must be equally capable. Their knowledge of the astronauts, their spacecraft, and the mission was crucial to success.

The same logic applies to building prosperous communities. Success is more likely when teams that are knowledgeable and supportive of the mission back community and economic development professionals and others working on the frontlines. Who are the support teams for community prosperity? The short answer is that all residents should work to make their community a better place, but key mission team members such as elected officials, civic board members, and other community leaders can spearhead the effort. And, as in space exploration, the more that community residents and team members know about community and economic development, the more likely the mission of community prosperity will succeed.

Our book *An Introduction to Community Development,* published by Routledge in 2009 with a second edition in 2015, was primarily intended to be used as a textbook for community and economic development courses. However, it was also purchased by a variety of users outside of the academic market. Several of the purchasers told us they bought the book because it was a good blend of theory, principles, and practice. The book was well received in part, we believe, because of this blend. One journal reviewer referred to us as "pracademics," a badge we wear proudly.

During the past few years, we have received a number of requests to write a book for the "support" team members—elected officials, board members, stakeholders, and citizens of all stripes who want to improve their community. We hope this book will fulfill those requests. A mirror image of *An Introduction to Community Development,* this book is primarily a "how to" guide for building prosperous communities, with just a pinch of theory thrown in to explain the principles. When it comes to building prosperous communities, good leaders can get you into orbit, but good leaders knowledgeable about community and economic development can get you to the moon.

We are fortunate to have been involved in community and economic development from a broad range of perspectives including teaching and research, consulting and actual practice. While research is growing and generating many useful results, community and economic development are still applied disciplines where much is learned through experience. The Janus Institute (janusinstitute.org), sponsor of the Janus Forum, which brings community and economic development professionals and community leaders together for peer learning and networking, and Rock Paper Scissors, a cutting-edge branding and marketing firm, have partnered to launch ProsperousPlaces.org as a resource to help communities create their roadmaps to prosperity. The website is an extension of this book, offering additional tools and shared knowledge to help communities move forward. We will update the site and travel with you along your community's road to prosperity.

We would like to thank our publisher Business Expert Press for recognizing the value and need for this book. BEP personnel are a pleasure to work with. Our thanks also to staff members who created the figures and illustrations in the book, assisted with research, proofed and cleaned up the manuscript, and helped in many other ways—from Rock Paper Scissors: Valerie Kinney, Kaitlin Henre, and Kimmie Zlatunich; and from Piedmont University: Cindy Nimmo. Piedmont University in Demorest, Georgia, provides support to the Janus Institute for which we are very grateful.

We would also like to acknowledge our families and friends who encouraged us through the laborious and time-intensive process of writing a book. We convey to them our thanks but also the bad news that we will undoubtedly be back at it again soon.

Robert H. Pittman
Rhonda Phillips
Amanda Sutt

Introduction

Welcome aboard the journey to community prosperity! The places we live affect our lives in many ways. Local employers provide jobs and incomes. Local governments build and maintain infrastructure and provide critical services such as fire and police protection. Communities educate our children and offer shopping, dining, entertainment, and recreational opportunities. Our families, friends, colleagues, and neighbors share the community with us.

Communities help define us. If someone sitting next to you on an airplane trip is from Manhattan, your preconceived notion of that person might well be urban sophisticate—business executive or arts and theater patron. If the person is from a small town in Montana, outdoor recreation or ranching might first come to mind. These preconceived notions may or may not be accurate, but they can influence how others perceive us.

Communities shape us as well. If the Manhattan resident inherits a ranch and moves to rural Montana, he or she might lose some of those big city ways and perhaps learn to hunt and fish. Conversely, if the small town Montana resident moves to Manhattan for the job of a lifetime, he or she will likely adapt to the faster pace of city living, learn to navigate public transportation, and enjoy the arts and theater. In a new environment, most people want to blend in, not stand out, and they tend to adopt some of the local culture.

Because the communities we live in are so important to us, we want to maintain and improve them not only for our own benefit but also for the benefit of family members and friends we share them with. When something good happens to our community such as a new business or downtown renovation, we take pride in the progress. However, when bad things happen such as the loss of a major employer, there can be mixed reactions. Some people may take the attitude that the town is on a downward path. Drive around the country and you will see many communities that are shadows of their former selves with vacant buildings and houses in disrepair. Other communities, however, are able to recover from setbacks and, if necessary, reinvent or "reboot" themselves. They are blessed with people who can adapt to change, roll up their sleeves, and work for a better future. And, communities of all sizes from small towns to sprawling metropolises can reboot and revitalize.

Consider, for example, Colquitt, Georgia, a small town of about 2,000 residents in the southwest part of the state. When, years ago, the agriculture industry there began a steady decline, the town's heritage and prosperity were threatened. "We realized we had to do something different if we were going to stay alive ... we were treading water," stated the city manager. Today, Colquitt is a popular tourist destination attracting thousands of visitors each year generating an economic impact of $2 million dollars.[1] The rest of the story of the transformation of Colquitt from a small farming town to a nationally known folk theater community whose "Swamp Gravy" production has played in Washington's Kennedy Center is offered at the end of the Introduction.

We wrote this book to help communities move forward. It's about place making and helping a community rebuild and reboot, making an already prosperous place even better, or achieving whatever outcome is desired by those who live there. We hope you find it entertaining as well as informative, and we wish you best wishes on your journey to community prosperity!

What Will You Learn?

Thomas Edison is credited with saying, "success is 90 percent perspiration and 10 percent inspiration." While that may be true for his inventions, we would assign more equal weights to success for community development and prosperity. Without a doubt, perspiration or hard work is a key component. Community progress does not occur overnight. It is almost always the result of determination and hard work by a wide group of leaders and citizens. Inspiration is also a key component. Communities that are motivated to overcome challenges, or by their vision of a better life for current and future generations, are certainly more likely to achieve

---

[1] 2021. "The Small But Mighty City of Colquitt Doesn't Quit," *Icma.Org.* https://icma.org/blog-posts/small-mighty-city-colquitt-doesnt-quit

prosperity than communities that believe their future will be determined by outside forces largely beyond their control. Combining this inspiration with an understanding of community and economic development principles creates a potent formula for community improvement.

Our primary objective for this book is to provide readers with a toolbox for community prosperity. The tools include:

 SUCCESS STORIES: Case studies and examples of how communities have achieved and maintained prosperity;

 ASSESSMENT: Understanding the current status of your community and identifying assets to build on and liabilities to address;

 VISIONING AND PLANNING: Creating a vision and plan for the future;

 LAYING THE FOUNDATION: Using community development best practices to build a "prosperous-ready" community that is an attractive business and residential location;

 BUILDING ON THE FOUNDATION: Using economic development best practices to create a strong economy and prosperous community;

 SUSTAINABILITY: Maintaining a prosperous community with better opportunities for all residents.

The COVID-19 pandemic has wreaked havoc around the world with business bankruptcies, mass unemployment, disruption of family life, and millions of deaths. Fortunately, vaccines were developed and rolled out in record time to support recovery from the pandemic. We would like to consider this book in a similar light. Understanding community and economic development principles and best practices can be a kind of vaccine to help communities cope with setbacks and remain healthy and prosperous.

Check In For Community Reboot Camp

reboot (rē-ˈbüt) : to start (something) anew: to refresh (something) by making a new start or creating a new version[2]

According to Merriam-Webster, the term reboot was first used in 1971 to describe restarting a computer to load a new operating system or fix a problem. Since then, it's become a regular part of our vocabulary. When one of the many electronic devices we constantly rely on seems to be confused and not working properly, our first reaction is usually to reboot, and, lo and behold, this frequently works for reasons the nontechnical among us can't explain. Reboot is now commonly used to describe a variety of situations involving transformation or starting afresh: rebooting companies, rebooting careers, or even rebooting relationships. Somehow rebooting seems to have a softer, less-threatening connotation than starting over, and thanks to those resurgent electronic devices, seems to carry a higher promise of success. Providing a higher standard of living and quality of life for all residents is possible for any community through smart community and economic development practices, whether it involves a reboot or just some tweaks to an already healthy community.

As we begin, let's define terms. Community has many connotations. It can refer to a group of people that share a connection or interest of some kind wherever the individuals are located, such as a community of

---

[2] "Reboot," *Merriam-Webster (Merriam-Webster)*, www.merriam-webster.com/dictionary/reboot (accessed April 05, 2021).

antique automobile enthusiasts. In this book, we use community in the sense of a geographic place—a small town or a large city under a single municipal government. However, the principles and ideas in this book can apply to a neighborhood, a metro area or region encompassing many jurisdictions, or even a state—any geographic area that would support common community and economic development policies.

The COVID-19 Pandemic—A Catalyst and Backdrop for the Book

We have been meaning to write this book for some time now. Our experience in working with communities across the country and around the world, and our research and teaching have provided us with knowledge we want to share with everyone interested in community and economic development—full-time professionals, elected officials, local board members, and community volunteers. Each community is unique, but the tried and true formulas for successful community and economic development still apply.

The COVID-19 pandemic acted as a catalyst encouraging us to put this book together at a time when economic and social disruption and tragic personal loss at both the global and local levels have been vividly and painfully demonstrated. Rebooting from this historic shock has taxed our political and social systems—indeed the human psyche—to their limits. However, tragedy and loss often make us thankful for things we might have taken for granted. We are all deeply indebted to our health care and public safety professionals for their unselfish and often heroic response to the pandemic.

Fortunately, as we write this book, recovery from the pandemic has occurred in the United States and around the world. However, variations of the coronavirus continue to pop up in different parts of the world, so the threat of new outbreaks remains. Despite the recovery from COVID-19, our research indicates that there will be lasting effects for many businesses, individuals and communities. Thousands of U.S. businesses have permanently closed, particularly in the hospitality and service industries. The shift to remote work caused by the pandemic has demonstrated to many companies and employees that commuting to the office daily and traveling for face-to-face meetings may no longer be the best business model. There are indications that increased reliance on remote work will be an enduring legacy of the pandemic with significant long-term implications for the travel and hospitality industries, commercial real estate markets, and businesses and residential locations. These effects will require significant adjustments for those parties most affected by the pandemic.

The immediate and severe impact of the COVID-19 pandemic prompted an extraordinary response from governments, businesses, and other private-sector organizations to address the public health and economic effects of the outbreak. At the local level, chambers of commerce, community and economic development agencies, and other public and private organizations in many communities reacted swiftly to help local businesses. Respondents to a ProsperousPlaces.org survey reported a variety of services that community and economic development agencies offered local businesses including serving as a clearinghouse for assistance information; facilitating communications among local organizations; and providing information on the status of local restaurant and retail establishments.[3]

In other words, people in towns and cities everywhere worked together to address a common problem and help their communities. This is the essence of the community development process that we will explore in detail in this book. Ironically, an unexpected benefit of the pandemic is an enhanced awareness and spirit of cooperation for community and economic development. Furthermore, as the saying goes, where there is change, there is new opportunity. While social and economic impacts from the pandemic such as increased reliance on remote work may present challenges for some cities, they may present opportunities for others. Both can best be addressed using community and economic development principles.

---

[3] N.A. October 13, 2020. "Economic Development in the New Normal," *ProsperousPlaces.org*, www.prosperousplaces.org/2020/09/14/economic-development-in-the-new-normal/

Change Comes in All Sizes and Flavors

Someone once said (and we're sure many people have taken credit for it) that the only certainty is uncertainty. The sudden onset of COVID-19 and its tremendous impacts caught the world by surprise. However, at any time communities of any size can be hit by shocks that for them are equal to or worse than the pandemic: industries decline, large companies shut down and lay off hundreds of workers, military bases close, major projects are cancelled—and the list goes on. Change can be sudden and dramatic, or it can be prolonged and subtle. In Douglas, Georgia, a local food processing plant shut down in May 2009 eliminating 2,200 jobs in a town with a population of 11,500. The county unemployment rate soared to 19 percent.[4] Cities like Allentown, Pennsylvania, and Duluth, Minnesota, lost thousands of jobs over several years as major industries undergirding their local economies declined (steel and mining, respectively).[5] Smaller towns such as Osceola, Arkansas, and Helper, Utah, lost major employers causing severe economic dislocation. Yet these and other cities that suffered major setbacks managed to reboot themselves, recover, and thrive. Tupelo, Mississippi, did not experience such sudden and dramatic shocks, but it successfully adapted to longer-term economic change and created local prosperity with a modern diversified economy. We will share the success stories of these communities and others throughout the book.

Central to the book is the question of why some communities thrive and grow while others stagnate or decline, and how some communities are able to reboot and recover from adversity or simply achieve their vision of becoming a better place to live, work, and play. Is there a secret sauce or fairy dust that makes communities successful and prosperous? What are the ingredients? Spoiler alert: no magic required, just good planning and execution and plenty of hard work—and any community can do it.

---

[4] "Turnaround Towns: International Evidence," *Carnegie UK Trust*, www .carnegieuktrust.org.uk/publications/turnaround-towns-international-evidence/ (accessed April 05, 2021).

[5] "Turnaround Towns: International Evidence," *Carnegie UK Trust*.

Some may say that communities should stick to the limited role of providing basic services such as public safety and municipal utilities and leave "prosperity" to the private sector. To that, we respond that a community is much more than streets and sewers. Individuals and businesses don't maintain their own parks and symphony halls. Through elected representatives, the residents of a community make collective decisions on publicly funded and shared services and amenities that define a community as much or more than basic services. While businesses and other job-creating organizations require good basic services to operate, they are also attracted to communities that have a good education system, reasonable regulatory policies, and quality of life amenities. Making a community more supportive of businesses and working to attract them in order to provide good jobs to residents is a time-honored and legitimate function for local governments and economic development organizations.

Who Should Read the Book?

If you have reached this section, either you have read the first few pages, or you are just skimming through looking for highlights and deciding whether you want to read the entire book. In either case, you must have an interest in community and economic development, and we wrote this book for you. A central theme is that community change and improvement is a team effort. When speaking or teaching, the authors are often asked, "How does my community get on the radar screen to attract new businesses and residents?" How to answer that in one minute or less? What's the elevator speech or soundbite for this question? After years of struggling to find a quick but meaningful answer instead of "it depends on the situation," our response now is "the more people that understand the fundamentals of community and economic development, the greater the chance of community improvement and greater prosperity."

Therefore, building awareness of community and economic development best practices and success stories is the raison d'etre for this book. It is written for community leaders, volunteers, and anybody interested in community improvement and progress, including professionals who work for community and economic development organizations. Even though these professionals may already be familiar with key concepts of community and economic development, our hope is that this book will enhance their knowledge. All in all, this book is aimed at a broad audience of community leaders because success in community and economic development requires a committed team.

Leadership does not just include elected officials. Community leaders, people who are listened to and respected for their civic commitment and work, commonly include executives from local businesses or community service organizations, members of local boards, or just volunteers who care about their community. What constitutes good leadership has been the subject of countless books, articles, and seminars. While it is not the primary focus of this book, we will consider leadership within the context of community and economic development.

How This Book Is Structured

While both research and practice in the field of community and economic development are constantly evolving, communities have been using these principles for decades to improve themselves. The effects of the COVID-19 pandemic, however, have made communities more aware of the importance of community and economic development and therefore created an enhanced learning opportunity. Chapter 1, The *New,* New Normal, puts the COVID-19 pandemic in historical perspective from a community and economic development standpoint and discusses how some pandemic-related changes are likely to persist, offering both challenges and opportunities for communities. Many people think of prosperity in only economic terms, but Chapter 2, How Prosperous is Your Community?, introduces a broader, holistic definition of prosperity and offers a roadmap to help attain it. Chapter 3, Laying the Foundation: A Prosperous-Ready Community, introduces the process of community development as a tool to position your community for prosperity. Chapter 4, Building a Prosperous Community, focuses on how economic development best practices, building on the foundation of Chapter 3, can help achieve prosperity. Chapter 5, Sustaining a Prosperous Community, summarizes some key lessons and presents more inspiring examples of successful communities.

How to Use This Book

Of course, you are free to surf and focus on the sections that most interest you, but the book is laid out sequentially and each chapter builds on previous ones. Just as a play would have less meaning if you missed Act One, skipping the initial chapters will diminish the essential message that community development is an important prerequisite to economic development and prosperity. Failure to understand and act on this is a major reason some communities are not as prosperous as others are. Community success involves subtle blends of knowledge and action, and we have attempted to present a balance of these elements. This book, then, is a call to action, but not to uninformed action. We do not advocate a "fire, ready, aim" approach.

To get the most out of this book, we suggest the following formula:

Read, Reflect, Share, and Act

Read: Learn principles and techniques and see how other communities have succeeded. Even if you are experienced in community and economic development, there will likely be some new ideas for you in the book.

Reflect: How do these principles, techniques, and examples apply to your community?

Share: Encourage others in your community to read and discuss the book. One person alone cannot generate community prosperity. Progress begins with a critical mass of informed local citizens and stakeholders.

Act: Each chapter concludes with a toolbox of action items based on that chapter's core principles. Let this book and other educational resources guide your community to effective action.

Community development is an ongoing process. The social, political, and economic circumstances surrounding a community change, sometimes gradually and sometimes suddenly like the COVID-19 pandemic. Circumstances within a community and its vision and goals also change. This book offers a toolbox to help communities get started on the journey to prosperity. It is designed to be a companion to additional resources available at ProsperousPlaces.org. Through programs created previously by the authors such as the Janus Forum (www.janusinstitute.org), we have seen first-hand the effectiveness of peer learning and shared experiences. Our goal is to create a "community of communities" to learn and grow with each other. We look forward to accompanying you on your journey to community prosperity, so turn to Chapter 1 and let's get started.

Prosperous Community Toolbox

The introduction to *How to Build Prosperous Places* sets the stage and explains why the book is particularly relevant in today's world. From global pandemics to businesses shutting their doors and eliminating thousands of jobs, there are many reasons why a community might need to adapt or reboot. Through this book and the accompanying worksheets, we'll explore ways anyone who cares about the place they call home can help lead the way to more prosperous tomorrows.

I.1 Encourage others in your community to read the book and learn more about community and economic development. To support this, we have set up bulk purchasing options to make it easier for you to share this with your fellow community members. Visit www.prosperousplaces. org/bulk to share.

I.2 Establish Community Action Groups. with regular meetings (in-person or virtual, depending on the situation and preference in your community) to discuss key concepts in the book, how they apply to your community, and how to begin the journey to community prosperity. Visit www.prosperousplaces.org/rebooteconomics_toolbox/ to download our tips for Community Actions Groups.

Colquitt, Georgia: Rebooting With Arts and Tourism

Figure I.1 Colquitt, Georgia

Who would have thought a small rural town with only vestiges of its former agricultural strength remaining would become a home for world-class storytelling? Well, that's exactly what Colquitt, Georgia (Figure I.1), did, converting an old cotton warehouse into a theater for sharing their stories and attracting tourists from around the world. To save their community as its agricultural industry declined, Colquitt community leaders knew they had to reboot. In this case, the proverb that necessity was the mother of invention was applicable.

Creating an art industry began as an idea of how to re-create and rebrand our community according to Cory Thomas, City Manager.[6] Individuals in the community "gathered stories of their heritage, history, and community to put on the stage," and the result was *Swamp Gravy*, named after a local stew. Swamp Gravy's mission is to "involve as many people as possible in a theatrical experience that empowers the individual, bonds the community and strengthens the local economy while crossing the boundaries of, race, economy and social class." As discussed in this book, this is the very essence of community and economic development.

Renovation of a cotton warehouse into a theater building was just the start of a downtown renaissance. According to one study, over $1 million has been invested in renovation and building projects, including a childcare center and storytelling museum patterned after the town square.[7] The Swamp Gravy Institute, which grew out of the revitalization initiative, holds workshops and helps other communities create their own productions. The Institute also sponsors an annual film festival and an after school program. Swamp Gravy has been performed in Centennial Park in Atlanta during the 1996 Olympics and at the Kennedy Center in Washington, DC. Swamp Gravy and associated initiatives have created jobs and generated millions of dollars in revenue for the city and county. Swamp Gravy is an inspiring example of the community development process with residents taking action to create arts-based economic development.

[6] N.A. 2021. "The Small But Mighty City Of Colquitt Doesn't Quit," *Icma. Org,* https://icma.org/blog-posts/small-mighty-city-colquitt-doesnt-quit
[7] N.A. 2021. "The Small But Mighty City Of Colquitt Doesn't Quit," *Icma. Org,* https://icma.org/blog-posts/small-mighty-city-colquitt-doesnt-quit

Ingredients for Swamp Gravy:
- 5 large potatoes, finely diced
- 1 large white onion, finely chopped
- 2 cups of whole kernel corn
- 14 oz. of cut okra
- 28 oz. of water
- 28 oz. of crushed red tomatoes
- Fish stock
- Full recipe: https://recipeself.com/swamp-gravy-recipe/

CHAPTER 1

A New "New Normal"?

Change is certain ... such recurrences should not constitute occasions for sadness but realities for awareness ...
Nothing is so painful to the human mind as a great and sudden change.

You might think these contrasting views on change must have been expressed by two people of different cultures living far apart; but in fact, they were married to each other. The first phrase was penned by English poet Percy Shelley during his short lifetime from 1792 to 1822, and the second phrase comes from his wife Mary Shelley's first edition of the novel *Frankenstein* published in 1818 (Figure 1.1).

Figure 1.1 Mary Shelley and Percy Shelley—Different views on change

Source: https://lithub.com/the-treacherous-start-to-mary-and-percy-shelleys-marriage/

Borrowing from medical terminology, Percy Shelley seems to be describing chronic or ongoing change while his wife, Mary, seems to be referring to acute or sudden change. Communities incur both types of change. One town could face continuous development pressures from a nearby larger city and another could suddenly lose a major employer. Change can, and should, also come from within—a desire for self-improvement. Whether change is fast or slow, severe or mild, or internal or external, there is much wisdom in Percy Shelley's words that change should create "realities for awareness." In the context of this book, it means that communities should be prepared to adapt and benefit from change.

From Change to New Normal

Acute and chronic can be useful terms for characterizing and understanding change; but sometimes, generational events such as the COVID-19 pandemic come roaring in so fast and hard that only words such as tsunami can describe them. The pandemic affected countries around the world and the communities within them. When a change of this magnitude occurs, the term "new normal" usually comes into play. New normal is a pretty serious phrase because it implies a significant change in our usual customs and routines. Dictionary.com defines new normal as "a current situation, social custom, etc., that is different from what has been experienced or done before but is expected to become usual or typical." According to this definition, there are two aspects of a new normal: significance and longevity.

Internet searches for the phrase "COVID-19 new normal" (in Summer 2021) generated 1.93 billion results (Figure 1.2). If web search hits are any indication of the relative importance placed on events or issues

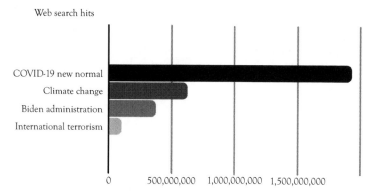

Figure 1.2 Web Searches: COVID-19 New Normal vs. Others

by the public, then the COVID-19 pandemic and its impact on how we live our daily life far outscores climate change (622 million hits), Biden Administration (371 million hits), and international terrorism (102 million hits).

New normal terminology is not unique to the COVID-19 pandemic. It has long been applied to a variety of situations. In 1918, new normal was used to describe the impact of World War I: "we must divide our epoch into three periods: that of war, that of transition and that of the new normal."[1] It has been used to describe the aftermath of a variety of financial disruptions including the 1990s dot-com bubble and the 2008 financial crisis and recession, and it has been applied to political transitions and new administrations. *New Normal* was even the title of a sitcom that aired on NBC from 2012 to 2013.

The Russian invasion of Ukraine in February 2022 is a recent example of a potentially long-term global political new normal. The invasion prompted a host of countries, including the United States and many European countries, to rethink their postwar foreign policies and impose economic sanctions on Russia to counter its military action. NATO Secretary-General Jens Stoltenberg stated that "It's obvious that we are faced with a new reality, a new security environment, a new normal.[2]"

Realizing that the term new normal is not unique to the COVID-19 pandemic raises several questions. When the term new normal is used, is the change really just a temporary aberration or something that will have a longer-lasting impact and therefore meet both aspects of the previously mentioned definition? How significant are the social, economic, and other changes in the new normal? How widespread are its effects across geographic and socioeconomic lines? Do we create categories for classifying new normals the way we do for hurricanes?

---

[1] H. Wood. 1918. A Wise, "Beware!" in *N.E.L.A. Bulletin* 5, pp. 604–605, National Electric Light Association.

[2] www.politico.com/news/2022/03/09/new-normal-forces-nato-rethink-security-00015714

Impacts of the COVID-19 Pandemic

The social and economic impact of the COVID-19 pandemic was swift and historically significant as shown in this partial timeline of U.S. events (Figure 1.3).

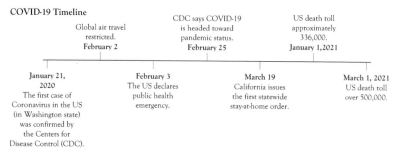

COVID-19 Timeline

Global air travel restricted. February 2	CDC says COVID-19 is headed toward pandemic status. February 25	US death toll approximately 336,000. January 1,2021
January 21, 2020 The first case of Coronavirus in the US (in Washington state) was confirmed by the Centers for Disease Control (CDC).	February 3 The US declares public health emergency.	March 19 California issues the first statewide stay-at-home order.

March 1, 2021
US death toll over 500,000.

Figure 1.3 COVID-19 timeline

Figure 1.4 shows how quickly and deeply the economic impact of the COVID-19 pandemic hit the United States.[3]

A June 2020 survey by ProsperousPlaces.org of local community and economic development professionals found that on average 48 percent of retail/restaurant businesses and 17 percent of all other businesses including manufacturing firms were closed in the respondents' communities as a result of the pandemic.[4]

Globally, the overall economic impact was equally significant. According to the United Nations Department of Economic and Social Affairs, the global GDP growth rate for 2020 was negative 5.0 percent, and the UN predicts that it will take several years to return to prepandemic levels. The world economy is expected to lose 8.5 trillion dollars in output for the two-year period from 2021 to 2022, erasing almost all of the increase

---

[3] N.A. April 01, 2021, "2021 State of the Union Facts," *USAFacts*, https://usa-facts.org/state-of-the-union/

[4] N.A. October 13, 2020. "Economic Development in the New Normal," *ProsperousPlaces.org*, www.prosperousplaces.org/2020/09/14/economic-develop-ment-in-the-new-normal/

COVID-19 impact infographic

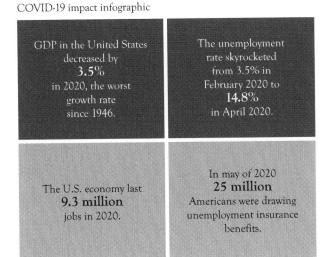

Figure 1.4 COVID-19 economic impact in the United States

for the previous four years and representing the sharpest contraction since the Great Depression in the 1930s.[5]

The COVID-19 downturn affected industries and regions in different ways and with varying degrees of severity. The travel industry experienced a 42 percent decline in revenue in 2020,[6] but the online shopping industry thrived, with Amazon reporting a 37 percent increase in sales for 2020 over 2019.[7] A study by the Brookings Institute compared the different impacts of the COVID-19 pandemic on industries and cities that rely on the movement of people with those that rely on the movement of

[5] "COVID-19 to Slash Global Economic Output by $8.5 Trillion over next Two Years | UN DESA Department of Economic and Social Affairs," United Nations (United Nations), www.un.org/development/desa/en/news/policy/wesp-mid-2020-report.html (accessed April 05, 2021).

[6] Ncarpenter@ustravel.org. February 25, 2021. "COVID-19 Travel Industry Research," U.S. Travel Association, www.ustravel.org/toolbox/covid-19-travel-industry-research

[7] N.A. February 2, 2021. "Amazon Profits Increased Nearly 200% with COVID-19: Research FDI," ResearchFDI https://researchfdi.com/amazon-covid-19-pandemic-profits/

information.[8] As the accompanying box shows, Las Vegas and Orlando, whose respective gaming and tourism economies rely more on the movement of people, were much harder hit by the pandemic than was Seattle with its software and information technology industries. Unfortunately, the COVID-19 pandemic had a disproportionate impact on minorities in many areas because of their higher employment concentrations in industries more affected by the downturn.

Some Cities and Workers Hit Harder by Pandemic

Las Vegas, Nevada's, core industries of gaming, tourism, and conventions rely heavily on the movement of people in and out of the city and the pandemic hit it hard. In the twelve-month period between November 2019 and November 2020 which includes the onset of the COVID-19 virus in the United States in the spring of 2020, the unemployment rate in the Las Vegas-Henderson-Paradise metropolitan area increased from 3.6 to 11.5 percent.

In the Orlando-Kissimmee-Sanford, Florida metropolitan area, another region that relies heavily on tourism, the unemployment rate increased from 2.7 to 7.7 percent during that same 12-month period. As a benchmark, the unemployment rate for the United States as a whole increased from 3.3 to 6.1 percent during that time, and, as noted earlier, spiked in April 2020 to 14.8 percent, remaining in double digits through July 2020.

---

[8] A. Klein, and E. Smith. February 05, 2021. "Explaining the Economic Impact of COVID-19: Core Industries and the Hispanic Workforce," *Brookings,* www .brookings.edu/research/explaining-the-economic-impact-of-covid-19-core-industries-and-the-hispanic-workforce/

In Las Vegas and Orlando, the shares of employment accounted for by the leisure and hospitality sectors that rely on moving people are relatively high (28 and 21 percent, respectively); however, the shares of employment accounted for by the professional and business service sectors that rely more on moving and processing information in these cities are relatively low (15 and 18 percent, respectively). By contrast, in the Seattle, Washington metro area, more of an information and goods moving region known for software and aviation products, the unemployment rate increased by only 2.1 percentage points from 3 percent in November 2019 to 5.1 percent in November 2020.

According to the Brookings study, in Las Vegas, Hispanic or Latino workers account for almost 25 percent of employment in the leisure and hospitality sectors with more person-to-person contact and less than 15 percent in the financial and information sectors. COVID-19 cases per 1,000 residents in the Las Vegas metro area were therefore much higher among Hispanic or Latino residents than white residents. On an age-adjusted basis, the COVID-19 death rates at the state level in Nevada for Hispanic or Latino residents through January 2021 were three times greater than those for white residents. The Brookings study provides a framework for understanding the differential impact of the COVID-19 pandemic on industries, cities, and ethnic groups. Such an analysis can help elected officials and policy makers at the national and local levels make more informed and equitable pandemic recovery decisions.

A Mega New Normal?

If new normal can be used to describe the aftermath of a sudden and distinct event such as a pandemic, financial crisis, or even war, then why can't it also be applied to more gradual but equally significant events and trends—sometimes referred to as long-wave changes? The case can be made that technological innovations over the past few decades have created a "mega" new normal. *Culture and Creativity* offers an assessment of some highly significant but more gradual changes that have occurred in recent years in the new age of instant communications:

Terrorism, war, new technologies, rapid political take-offs and no less rapid falls—we saw pretty much the same things in the 1960s, the 1970s, the 1980s, and the 1990s. Significant changes able to shape a nation or change a society happened in long waves encompassing entire generations and not just decades. Indeed, the most significant trends of the 2010s were already very visible in 1999 or even 1989. Still, some long-wave trends have greatly accelerated during the last 15 years.

The most significant acceleration can be observed in communication technologies. According to the latest data, in 2015 the number of mobile communications users exceeded 7 billion people while in 2000 their number was just about one billion. Not only urban but also rural residents use Wi-Fi. They can reach any place in the world from the comfort of their own homes.

The 2000s saw the emergence of technologies able to strengthen our relations. In 2010, Facebook became the most visited website, even though in 2000 it simply did not exist. The same trends can be observed in modern mobile communications technologies. They do not try to replace our personal communication. Instead, they aim to extend and deepen our communication opportunities for keeping in touch with people far away.[9]

In addition to providing individuals with personal communication links around the world, mobile devices enable us to instantly retrieve information, answer questions, or get directions to the nearest Mexican restaurant in seconds. Social media sites have also revolutionized personal communications and the way we receive and disseminate information. Of course, all this is made possible by the Grand Master of the change parade over the last few decades—the Internet. Instant communications and information and countless other innovations made possible by the Internet have created what can legitimately be termed a "mega new normal."

---

[9] "Your Editorial on Culture & Creativity," April 30, 2018, www.culturepartnership .eu/en/article/top-9-trends-of-the-last-decade

Long-wave changes such as the Internet's impacts on information and communication, unfold over years or decades. While it can be harder to comprehend their full nature and ultimate impacts, at least we have time to adapt to them. On the other hand, the COVID-19 pandemic struck virtually overnight and peaked in a few weeks, making it painfully obvious but more difficult to respond to so quickly. Communities face these challenges constantly. Events such as the loss of a major employer with economic and social impacts comparable to the pandemic can happen any time to a community. As case studies and examples in this book show, cities or regions prepared to respond to these shocks using the tools of good community and economic development can rebound and, if necessary, reboot more quickly and successfully than communities caught unprepared can. Using tools such as community assessments and strategic planning, these communities are positioned better to respond to both short- and longer-term changes.

Rebooting Downtown Allentown, Pennsylvania

When traditional employers including Bethlehem Steel and Mack Trucks closed or downsized, Allentown fell from prosperity into decline. The downtown retail district, which included the popular Hess department store, was particularly hard hit, and pawnshops and boarded up storefronts started to proliferate. This spurred planning and cooperation between the public and private sectors, and, with support from the state, downtown Allentown underwent a renaissance. The City Center area now features a hockey arena, new office space, museums, art galleries, and a growing residential sector.

A catalyst for the renaissance of downtown was the creation of a Neighborhood Improvement Zone (NIZ) through legislation passed by the state in 2009. Under this program, nonproperty state and local taxes generated in the 130-acre downtown NIZ are invested back into the area instead of going to state and local general revenue coffers. Some of this money is used to subsidize private sector development, which allows developers to charge lower rents, thus attracting businesses and residents to the downtown area. The NIZ money also helps support public services in the area. The NIZ program has helped bring thousands of new jobs and over $1 billion in investment to City Center Allentown. The jobs vary from entry-level positions in the retail and hospitality sectors to professional jobs in companies such as the Lehigh Valley Health Network, CrossAmerica Partners, and the BB&T (now Truist) Corporation.

The Urban Land Institute cited the renaissance of downtown Allentown as an excellent example of success through public-private collaboration, strong leadership, entrepreneurial spirit, and a clear vision for the future. Local and state politicians set aside differences to help make the NIZ program a success. "Partisanship has to be set aside if we're going to solve the problems of challenged cities," stated one elected official. *US News* now ranks Allentown as one of the eight best places to live in Pennsylvania. The Allentown story is a good illustration of a community pulling together to address the problems brought on by the decline of local industries and other adverse trends. Allentown adjusted to its own "new normal" and forged a path toward prosperity.[10]

From Pandemic to New Normal

Has the COVID-19 pandemic created a new normal? It would be questionable at this point to equate the effects of the pandemic to the long-wave transformational changes enabled by the Internet, but the COVID-19 saga is far from over. Variants that are even more infectious have appeared in places around the world and spread quickly. Some infectious disease experts have predicted that the COVID-19 virus and its variants will remain a significant public health threat for the foreseeable future. Furthermore, there is concern and speculation that long-term social and economic impacts of the pandemic could last for years or decades.

---

[10] J. Tierney. 2021. "Breathing Life Into Allentown: Pennsylvania Comes To The Rescue," *The Atlantic*, www.theatlantic.com/business/archive/2014/09/breathing-life-into-allentown-pennsylvania-comes-to-the-rescue/379742/ and N.A. 2021. "Turnaround Towns," *Carnegie UK Trust*, www.carnegieuktrust.org.uk/project/turnaround-towns

Generational Impacts

The COVID-19 pandemic had a pervasive impact on many aspects of society in countries around the globe. The millions of deaths and tremendous economic damage, including lost output, mass unemployment, and permanent business closures, are painfully obvious. Other impacts such as disruptions in education and mental health issues may not be as visible yet, but they may prove to be just as significant in the long run. The *Harvard Gazette* consulted faculty experts across specialties to help identify impacts of the pandemic that may continue to affect society long after the medical emergency subsides and economic output recovers.[11] Dr. Karestan Koenen, the professor of psychiatric epidemiology at the Harvard School of Public Health, cites several impacts of the pandemic on the "COVID-19 generation" with potential long-term effects:

- Uncertainty and uncontrollability regarding many of life's major milestones such as entering school, graduating, getting a job, and even getting married and having children.
- Physical distancing and isolation, encouraging people to rely more on social media and less on in-person socialization.
- Isolation and curtailed activities that interfere with developmental opportunities for young people to try new things, learn from experiences, and acquire new skills.

Dr. Koenen concludes that "While it's likely that the coming-of-age generation will bear long-term impacts (from the COVID-19 pandemic), it's less clear what those might be." She believes the pandemic's traumas could lead to a rise in hopelessness and higher levels of anxiety and depression that could continue for years to come. Furthermore, some people who have had the COVID-19 virus experience continuing long-term effects such as fatigue, lung problems, brain fog, and other symptoms.

---

[11] N.A. 2021. "Our Post-Pandemic World And What'S Likely To Hang Round," *Harvard Gazette*, https://news.harvard.edu/gazette/story/2020/11/our-post-pandemic-world-and-whats-likely-to-hang-round/

Economic Impacts: The Job Market and Labor Force

A report by the McKinsey Global Institute based on surveys of top business executives in eight large-economy countries provides useful insights into the potential long-term impacts of the pandemic on businesses and their employees.[12] As shown in the accompanying box, the report concludes that the COVID-19 pandemic accelerated three broad trends that could affect work and how it is done on a long-term basis: (1) the shift to remote work and virtual interactions; (2) a surge in e-commerce; and (3) the deployment of automation and artificial intelligence.

The Future of Work After COVID-19

This study by the McKinsey Global Institute classifies occupations and industries by the degree to which their operations require physical proximity and therefore less opportunity for decentralized or remote work. For example, occupations in the "work arenas" of health care, personal care, and retail had high physical proximity scores, while occupations involving computer office work, transportation of goods and outdoor production, and maintenance had low physical proximity scores. The study identified three long-term trends that could be a legacy of the COVID-19 Pandemic:

1. Shift to Remote work
   - *Only a portion of jobs lend themselves to remote work.* "Considering only remote work that can be done without a loss of productivity, we find that about 20 to 25 percent of the workforces in advanced economies could work from home between three and five days a week. Advanced economies, with a greater share of jobs in the computer-based office arena, have a higher potential for remote work than emerging economies."

[12] 2021. www.mckinsey.com/featured-insights/future-of-work/the-future-of-work-after-covid-19.https://www.mckinsey.com/featured-insights/future-of-work/the-future-of-work-after-covid-19

- *The share of all jobs that can be done remotely without loss of productivity is higher than before the pandemic.* Because of the forced learning curve, it is four to five times higher.
- *A reduced number of employees working in offices could have multiplier effects.* Thirty percent of executives surveyed by McKinsey planned to reduce office space by an average of 30 percent. With fewer regular office workers, the demand for nearby restaurants and retail and also public transportation may be negatively affected.
- *Where people do remote work could have significant but differing implications for cities and towns of all sizes.* The prepandemic trend of a disproportionate share (relative to population) of job growth going to large cities could be reversed. Office vacancy rates in 2020 increased by 91 percent in San Francisco and by 32 percent in London, while they declined in smaller cities such as Glasgow, Scotland, and Charlotte, North Carolina. Some companies are considering opening more satellite offices in lower-population areas to facilitate remote work and attract workers who live there.
- *The pandemic appears to have encouraged a migration in some areas from larger urban areas to smaller cities and urban areas.* Data from LinkedIn analyzed by McKinsey show that more members moved from larger cities to smaller cities in 2020 than in 2019. The LinkedIn data also show that large metro areas such as New York City; the San Francisco Bay Area; Washington, DC; and Boston had a greater decline in the inflow-outflow ratio than smaller cities such as Madison, Wisconsin, and Jacksonville, Florida.
- *The increased use of videoconferencing and other remote means of communications brought business travel to a virtual standstill* at the height of the pandemic, and it may not recover to prepandemic levels for several years. McKinsey estimates that a 20 percent decline in business travel may persist after economic recovery from the pandemic. This would have a lasting impact on travel-related industries.

2. Increased use of e-commerce and other virtual transactions.

- *In 2020, the share of e-commerce in retail sales grew* across their surveyed countries by a rate of two to five times the rate than before the pandemic. In the United States, its share grew by 4.6 percent compared to an annual average growth over 2015 to 2019 of 1.4 percent.

- *Significant growth during the pandemic has also occurred in virtual transactions* including telemedicine, online banking, and streaming entertainment. This trend has encouraged growth in jobs in sectors such as warehousing, transportation, and delivery while contributing to declines in in-store jobs such as cashiers. Some retailers such as Macy's and Gap are closing brick and mortar stores, but e-commerce related companies like Amazon are adding facilities and employees (400,000 hired during the pandemic).

- *These changes could lead to more gig or freelance workers* in these growing employment sectors. They may also have significant implications (positive or negative) for the economic health of communities who have larger numbers of workers in these affected sectors.

3. Faster adoption of automation and artificial intelligence

- *In periods of increased pressure to reduce operating costs such as recessions, research indicates that many businesses tend to adopt automation technologies and redesign work processes.* The McKinsey survey showed that two-thirds of the responding senior executives said they were stepping up automation and artificial intelligence in their operations.

- *An increasing trend toward automation and artificial intelligence* is likely to have a larger negative impact on lower-skilled workers.

The report goes on to identify the following potential impacts of this new normal on the labor force:

- *Almost one-third of the U.S. labor force will be more footloose, able to do most of their work effectively at remote*

locations. For the computer-based office work arena
(including occupations such as accountants, lawyers,
financial managers, and business executives) that accounts
for 31 percent of the U.S. labor force, the study estimates
that 70 percent of work time can be spent at remote
locations without losing effectiveness. In most other work
arenas more closely tied to a job site, as little as 5 to 10
percent of work can be effectively done remotely. The
upshot is that the COVID-19 new normal may feature a
different mix of occupations driven by the previous three
trends. The study predicts that by 2030, the share of total
employment in many countries will be higher compared
to the prepandemic situation in sectors such as health care
workers and STEM (Science, Technology, Engineering,
and Mathematics) workers and lower in occupations such
as office support, production and warehousing work, and
customer service and sales.

- *Almost all labor demand growth will be in high-wage
  occupations.* More low-wage workers will have to find
  new jobs, but since low-skill jobs will not be growing,
  many will have to transition to higher-skilled positions.
  This will require more social and emotional skills as well
  as technical skills and more occupation-specific training
  resources at the national and local levels.

Trends identified in the study such as migration from large urban
areas to rural and smaller metro areas along with development of tools to
facilitate remote work are game changers. If the pandemic has accelerated
these trends as the McKinsey study suggests, then it may have indeed
helped create a lasting new normal and pattern of work.

The New Geography of Work

In the time-honored real estate mantra "location, location, location," the
word is repeated to emphasize the advantages of *one* place. Perhaps now

we should repurpose the phrase to indicate the advantages of *three* related places—where the remote worker lives, where the boss lives, and where the physical office (if there is one) is located.

The McKinsey study offers compelling evidence that increased reliance on remote work may be a lasting legacy of the COVID-19 pandemic. Other surveys and studies support this conclusion. Corporate real estate executives and business location consultants are two groups of professionals positioned well to observe first-hand how the COVID-19 pandemic has influenced remote work and the use of company facilities. Corporate real estate executives manage a company's existing facilities and help plan for future office and production space requirements. Business location consultants help companies find the best locations for new facilities across countries, states, and communities.

CoreNet Global, a professional association of corporate real estate executives headquartered in Atlanta, surveyed its members in January 2021 concerning the lasting effects of the pandemic on work and facilities in some of the world's leading companies.[13] These findings are listed in the accompanying box.

CoreNet Global Survey on Effects of Pandemic on Remote Work and Corporate Facilities

Some key findings:

- **Decreased Corporate Footprint:** 33 percent of respondents project that by 2022 the company's overall real estate footprint will have shrunk by between 10 and 30 percent.
- **Work Hours:** 69 percent responded that the 9 to 5 work pattern is a thing of the past.
- **Hiring Remote Employees:** 57 percent responded that their companies would consider hiring employees regardless of location.

---

[13] N.A. February 10, 2021. "The Pandemic's Effect on Corporate Real Estate," *CoreNet Global News Release.*

- **Where the Work Will be Done:** On average, the respondents reported that in the future 46 percent of the typical work week will be in a traditional office, 43 percent at home or another remote location, and 11 percent in a co-working environment.
- **Corporate Satellite Locations:** 16 percent responded that their companies would be opening satellite offices closer to where employees live.
- **Reshoring:** 53 percent of respondents projected an increase in reshoring by their companies, with 81 percent reporting that it would occur in North America.

The CoreNet survey paints a picture of a postpandemic new normal where flexible remote work will be much more common, and new employees will not necessarily have to live within commuting distance from their offices. As a result, companies will need less space and will reduce their real estate footprint, and some will move closer to where their employees live. Under this new geography of work, company facilities and operations are likely to be more spread out and even follow their employees. This is certainly a movement away from the old model of companies and their workers locating in close proximity to each other to accommodate the daily commute. This traditional model encourages clustering of companies and employees in larger metropolitan areas and contributes to traffic congestion and air pollution.

A survey of business location consultants by *Site Selection* magazine in late December 2020 further illustrates the trend toward a new geography of work.[14] In an article aptly entitled "Instead of People Chasing Jobs, Jobs Are Now Chasing People," *Site Selection* reported that 83 percent of survey respondents indicated that increased reliance on remote work is

[14] R. Starner. n.d. "Site Selectors Survey: 5 Ways COVID-19 Changed Site Selection: Site Selection Magazine," Site Selection, https://siteselection.com/issues/2021/jan/site-selectors-survey-five-ways-covid-19-changed-site-selection.cfm (accessed April 05, 2021).

having some effect or a significant effect on the facility location decisions of their client companies. The *Site Selection* article states that "companies are realizing they no longer have to remain in large and costly city centers," citing the result that 51 percent of survey respondents said their companies were considering moving their business operations away from city centers to suburbs and rural locations.

Of course, the future is notorious for not accommodating predictions. The social and economic impacts of the COVID-19 pandemic and the new normal it might engender is subject to much speculation. The surveys and studies cited previously and others indicate that the social and economic impacts of the COVID-19 pandemic, possibly along with other trends already in the making, will help create a new geography of work with potentially significant changes in where work gets done and where companies and employees choose to locate. In fact, companies such as Nationwide, Twitter, and JPMorgan Chase have already introduced permanent work-from-home policies. The pandemic certainly created a new normal for work in the short run, and there is considerable evidence that it will have long-lasting effects in many sectors and areas.

Challenges and Opportunities for Communities

Janus is the Roman god symbolizing change and transition to a new state, such as from the past to the future or from one vision to another (Figure 1.5). Janus is associated with new doorways to the future and new opportunities, and that's why the first month of the year is called January.

He is usually depicted as having two faces, one looking backward to the past and the other to the future. Janus is a fitting symbol for community change and progress. Change brings uncertainty and usually some measure of risk. Therefore, some communities may be hesitant to embrace change and look for new opportunities. Sometimes, communities are afraid that a change will threaten their identity and heritage—the things that have made them unique. However, successful communities are able to blend change and new opportunity with the assets and characteristics that have served them well in the past. Just like Janus, they are looking toward the future with an appreciation for the past.

Figure 1.5 Janus: The Roman god of new beginnings

Source: www.britannica.com/topic/Janus-Roman-god

It is often said that change brings opportunities as well as challenges, and the COVID-19 pandemic is no exception. For less-populated areas— smaller cities and rural areas—there may be opportunities to gain benefits from the outmigration from larger metro areas. Mymove.com analyzed change-of-address data from the U.S. Postal Service to determine the extent and nature of the outmigration.[15] They found that in 2020, the year of the pandemic, 15.9 million people filed a change-of-address form, representing a nationwide increase of 4 percent over 2019. However, the data show that outmigration from major cities such as New York, Chicago, and San Francisco (Figure 1.6) was significantly higher in 2020 than in 2019. Outmigration increased in San Francisco by almost 300 percent in 2020 over 2019. On the other hand, cities where in-migration increased in 2020 over 2019 include smaller cities such as Katy, Texas (population 26,909); Meridian, Idaho (101,905); and Leander, Texas (75,976).

People move from larger cities to smaller ones for a host of reasons such as a lower cost of living and, for them, a better lifestyle. A recent survey by the Pew Research Center of 10,000 U.S. movers revealed that

---

[15] N.A. February 17, 2021. "Coronavirus Moving Study Shows More Than 15.9 Million People Moved During COVID-19," MYMOVE, www.mymove.com/moving/covid-19/coronavirus-moving-trends/

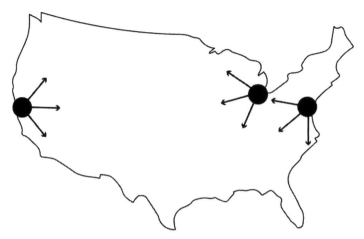

Figure 1.6 Outmigration from New York, Chicago, and San Francisco

28 percent cited fear of getting COVID-19 in their current location as the reason for moving and 18 percent cited financial reasons including job loss which, given the huge economic shock of the pandemic, might have been COVID-19 related.[16] Big Technology, a newsletter covering technology industries, analyzed the relocation patterns of technology workers to determine which cities had gains and which had losses in this important segment of the workforce.[17] Using inflow over outflow ratios as a measuring tool, they found that cities such as Madison, Wisconsin, and Hartford, Connecticut, had positive net inflows while cities such as Boston and the San Francisco Bay Area had positive net outflows. This relocation trend by tech workers probably reflects the decisions of some large employers such as Facebook and Google allowing some employees to work remotely on a permanent basis.

There is evidence that a trend away from big cities toward smaller cities and rural areas was gaining steam even before the COVID-19 pandemic.

---

[16] K. Alex. December 17, 2020. "Where Tech Workers Are Moving: New LinkedIn Data vs. the Narrative," *Big Technology*, https://bigtechnology.substack. com/p/where-tech-workers-are-moving-new

[17] C. D'Vera. January 13, 2021. "About a Fifth of U.S. Adults Moved Due to COVID-19 or Know Someone Who Did," *Pew Research Center*, www.pewresearch. org/fact-tank/2020/07/06/about-a-fifth-of-u-s-adults-moved-due-to-covid-19-or-know-someone-who-did/

In 2019, the Public Broadcasting System (PBS) cited data showing that collectively U.S. cities lost nearly 300,000 millennials in 2018—the fourth consecutive year that cities lost some of these productive workers aged 24 to 40.[18] The PBS also cited a 2018 Gallup Poll showing that two-thirds of respondents would prefer to live in a rural area, small city, or town, while only 12 percent would prefer to live in a big city.[19]

If more skilled workers are moving to smaller cities and rural areas, are companies following them? Unfortunately, data regarding the movement of employers are harder to obtain. Still, the surveys cited earlier from corporate real estate executives (CoreNet) and business location consultants (*Site Selection* magazine) indicated that many companies do expect to relocate away from metro areas to smaller cities and rural areas.

An increase in a community's workforce, especially skilled workers, can offer a community many potential economic development benefits. Local businesses will have a deeper and richer labor pool to draw from, and a community can become more attractive to companies looking for a new location. A growing population and expanding workforce contribute to the local economy through activities such as buying a home, eating in restaurants, and shopping in local retail stores. Furthermore, there are many examples of highly skilled workers such as engineers and computer scientists putting down roots and starting businesses in their new communities.

Recognizing the advantages of a robust labor supply, some communities have established programs to attract workers through incentives such as cash stipends, free co-working space, and housing allowances. The Northwest Arkansas Council offers $10,000 and a free bicycle to entice remote workers to move to Benton or Washington counties in the northwest part of the state. Most of these enticement

---

[18] "Why Millennials Are Moving Away From Large Urban Centers," 2021. *PBS Newshour*, www.pbs.org/newshour/show/why-millennials-are-moving-away-from-large-urban-centers

[19] Gallup, Inc. 2021. "Americans Big On Idea Of Living In The Country," *Gallup. Com*, https://news.gallup.com/poll/245249/americans-big-idea-living-country.aspx

programs are aimed at a particular audience, such as technology workers, and have specific qualification requirements. Hamilton, Ohio, will offer up to $10,000 to recent college graduates to move to certain parts of the city. Natchez, Mississippi, offers $6,000 to remote workers with their "Shift South" initiative to relocate to their historic city where housing prices are quite affordable in comparison to other parts of the United States. Other cities with worker recruitment programs include Tulsa, Oklahoma; Savannah, Georgia; Baltimore, Maryland; and New Haven, Connecticut. These programs target individuals with degrees in science, technology, engineering, or mathematics. Sometimes preference is given to those who have a desire to give back to the community through activities such as restoring a historic property or starting a new business.

Some states and countries (e.g., Vermont and Chile) also offer relocation incentives to targeted workers. Ironically, these worker attraction programs are the mirror image of the historical norm of offering incentives to entice companies to move to the community. More communities, states, and countries are realizing that building a strong workforce can be a better way to attract outside investment and encourage new enterprise startups. And if the speculation that more employers will be following people as a result of the new normal, then all the more reason to build a strong workforce.

Is Your Community Remote Work Friendly?

While the COVID-19 pandemic compelled many companies to temporarily adopt remote work where possible, many will continue the practice indefinitely because of newfound benefits to the employer and employee. Notably, leading technology companies such as Google and Apple have announced a permanent remote work model for some employees. As a result, companies and workers have more latitude in their locational choices. Many companies are now less tied to population centers and therefore can consider lower-cost locations. Workers are also freer to move to areas with a lower cost of living, better recreational opportunities, and other attributes they may prefer.

This new geography of work may provide community and economic development opportunities for some locations. Remote workers are often highly educated, well-paid professionals whose incomes and expenditures can help boost a local economy and create jobs. Likewise, remote work companies are often in growing knowledge-based service industries that can expand and diversify a local economy. Because of their appeal, attracting remote work companies and workers is highly competitive.

Communities that are remote work-friendly may be able to gain a competitive advantage in attracting remote work companies and workers. These places have good telecom service, endorse and encourage remote work, and offer a business community and workforce experienced in and supportive of remote work. Remote work-friendly should be demonstrated and preferably certified by an independent third party.

Community certification labels such as "development ready" or "available inventory of suitable sites and buildings" granted by states or independent organizations have proven to be a powerful economic development recruiting tool. In the competitive site selection process, certification in these areas can reduce perceived risk and put a community on the location shortlist more quickly. Similarly, communities can gain a competitive edge in the new normal world of remote work by attaining a remote work-friendly designation.

Embracing the Future

Amidst its chaos and tragedy, the COVID-19 pandemic has encouraged us to consider some challenging questions. How long will the social and economic disruptions caused by the pandemic continue around the world? How will the COVID-19 new normal evolve? What is the likelihood that other pandemics or major shocks (e.g., financial or political) will materialize? Despite our focus on recovering from the COVID-19 pandemic and on the possibility of future shocks, opportunities in the new, new normal world are gaining our attention. The new geography of work may contribute to prosperity in some communities through more footloose companies and remote workers moving to them. It can also encourage community improvement to attract these companies and workers (becoming remote work friendly), which also benefits current residents.

Global shocks such as the COVID-19 pandemic may be relatively rare, but local shocks such as the shutdowns of a major employer happen to some communities somewhere every day. They can occur without warning or they can be a predictable culmination of ongoing trends. The COVID-19 pandemic has served as a stark illustration that a change can occur anytime, and, hopefully, it has encouraged some communities to think about how to protect themselves from future disruptions and even leverage them to their advantage. Communities can prosper by creating a more diversified economy and becoming more adept at managing change.

The popular adage "if it ain't broke, don't fix it" is a colorful way of saying don't mess with success. But, success can be ephemeral. If you follow this rule, then you wait for things to break before you take any action. But, therein lies the problem—they break. This is a reactive strategy. Who would recommend waiting until a car engine seizes up or the brakes fail to check the oil and brake fluid? A much better prescription would be, "If it ain't broke, it will be, so you had better figure out how you're going to fix it." Better yet, "fix it before it breaks." In other words, plan and act proactively; don't just sit around waiting for the old normal to return because it might be gone forever.

How prepared is your community to cope with evolving economic and social trends, or better yet, take advantage of them? Do your elected officials, stakeholders, and fellow residents view change as an opportunity for growth and prosperity or as a Frankenstein monster? Has your community established a vision and plan for the future, or are you just drifting with the current, oblivious to the rapids and waterfalls ahead? In short, how prepared is your community to reboot and prosper? For most communities, prosperity is not anointed; it is earned by understanding and using the tools in the community and economic development best practices toolbox.

Prosperous Community Toolbox

Read, Reflect, Share, and Act

Chapter 1 is about change and how communities respond to it. Ironically, the COVID-19 pandemic served as a kind of fire drill showing communities everywhere what can happen almost overnight to disrupt the local economy. It is useful to reflect on how the actions taken to address the pandemic can serve as "lessons learned" for a better community response to future economic challenges. The goals of the tools for Chapter 1 are to assess how your community responded to the pandemic, and to assess small business assistance programs in your community and its remote work "friendliness" that can help with recovery and economic growth.

1.1 In your Community Action Groups, discuss and assess the ways the COVID-19 pandemic (or other crises) affected your community. Will there be long-term effects on your community? If so, what? What opportunities have been created? Do a self-assessment (conduct a community survey if you like) of how your community reacted to the COVID-19 pandemic. How did local governments, community and economic development agencies (including chambers of commerce) and other civic organizations participate?

1.2 Inventory the businesses recovery and assistance programs in your community. Does your community have small business assistance or mentoring programs? How can the community assist the owners/managers of closed businesses and other entrepreneurs to start new businesses?

1.3 Determine how remote work friendly your community is. Download our list of factors that help make a community remote work friendly. Use the list to get an idea for how remote work friendly your community is and how you can improve.

Visit https://www.prosperousplaces.org/rebooteconomics_toolbox/ to download the Chapter 1 tools.

CHAPTER 2

How Prosperous Is Your Community?

If you are fortunate enough to live in a nice neighborhood and have a good job, you probably feel some degree of prosperity. Other residents of your community may be as prosperous as you or more so, while some are struggling just to get by. But, overall, would you consider your community to be prosperous? If out-of-town friends came to visit and you took them on a tour showing them the neighborhoods, retail shops, restaurants, local industries, and other "good" parts of town, would it be hard to avoid the "bad" ones? Several years ago, a mayor gave a group of economic developers, including one of the authors, a tour of his small southern town. He pointed out historic homes, a new city hall, and scenic river vistas, but when he drove through a blighted part of town, he asked everyone in the tour van to lower their window shades for a promotional video—an enterprising, if amusing, approach to community marketing. To address the question of "how prosperous is your community?" we need to first define the term.

What Is Prosperity?

Prosperity is a word with many connotations. If you were to walk down a main street sidewalk and randomly ask passers-by to define prosperity, most people would probably mention wealth, a good job, and other aspects of economic success. You might also hear things such as a self-made person, a rising star, or terms similar to those found in various dictionary definitions of prosperity. Other respondents might have a much different perspective on prosperity. The Buddhist religion includes collectivism and spirituality in the definition of prosperity.[1] Yourdictionary.com

---

[1] R.S. Gottlieb. 2003. Essay. In *Liberating Faith: Religious Voices for Justice, Peace, and Ecological Wisdom* 288, Lanham, MD: Rowman & Littlefield Publishers.

defines prosperity as "the state of being wealthy, or having a rich and full life."[2] Note the "or" in this definition, implying that wealth and a rich and full life are not necessarily related and either one can be a path to prosperity. Most people, however, might believe that wealth without a rich and full life is a vacuous kind of prosperity.

Each of us can embrace our own definition of personal prosperity, but how do we define community prosperity? More to the point, how should a community define prosperity for itself? Most residents, assuming they do not seek a back-to-nature lifestyle, would probably include a strong local economy with good jobs and economic opportunity for all in their definition of community prosperity. But, is economic success alone enough to call a community prosperous? What about the "rich and full life" and "self-made" aaspects of prosperity in the aforementioned definitions?

A Tale of Two Cities

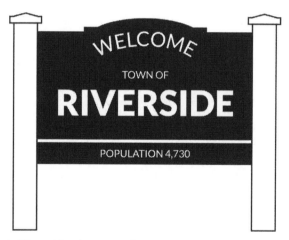

Figure 2.1 Riverside: A new tech town

Let's consider for a moment two towns: Riverside (Figure 2.1), where technology companies have moved in creating high-income jobs, and Port City (Figure 2.2), where growth is stagnant and lower-paying manual labor jobs prevail. Given only this information, you might consider Riverside to be the more prosperous community. But, let's do some fieldwork and find out more about them. From visits to these two towns, we

---

[2] www.yourdictionary.com/prosperity" (accessed April 12, 2021).

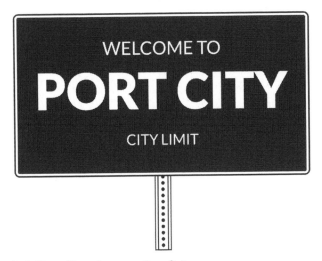

Figure 2.2 Port City: A town of tradition

discover that few residents of Riverside are involved in civic activities and there is little sense of community identity. On the other hand, Port City's residents are active in neighborhood and civic associations that sponsor community improvement projects, festivals, and concerts. People know each other, and there is a sense of community pride. The accompanying boxes paint a more detailed picture of these two contrasting towns.

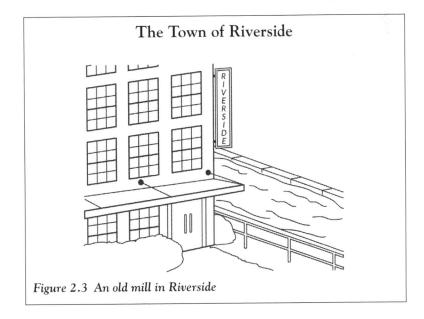

Figure 2.3 An old mill in Riverside

Riverside, founded over 150 years ago, grew up around manufacturing firms that originally located there because of hydropower. Over the last three decades, however, employment in Riverside's manufacturing sector steadily declined as many local firms moved overseas. The ones that stayed eventually succumbed to lower-cost competitors. Despite limited attempts at reuse, the stately old mills by the river eventually fell into disrepair, as did many other parts of the city. Many of Riverside's residents, watching their children leave for opportunity elsewhere, became discouraged and withdrew from community involvement or even moved away. While Riverside's economy declined, Danville, a larger city an hour's drive away, experienced a boom as technology companies grew nonstop, driving up occupancy costs and creating rush-hour traffic congestion. Looking for lower-cost locations but not wanting to abandon a skilled labor force, the owners and managers of Danville's high-tech firms discovered Riverside's old mills with their scenic river location and converted them into mixed-use production and office space (Figure 2.3).

The technology companies wanted to staff their new Riverside offices with local residents where possible, but few residents had the appropriate experience and skills, so they asked some of their current employees to transfer to Riverside. Some of these well-paid employees relocated to Riverside, but many others felt tied to Danville because of its good schools and quality of life and therefore chose to maintain their residence there and commute to work in Riverside. The employees that relocated to Riverside tended to cluster in several new gated communities on the west side of town closest to Danville. Riverside benefited from increased tax revenues from the renovated mills, new residential developments, and more daytime retail activity. As a result, the city was able to repair some aging infrastructure and improve its appearance. However, the civic commitment to Riverside from new technology workers was low and they did not get involved in community affairs. Instead, they maintained social ties in Danville and drove back there to visit friends, shop, and otherwise enjoy the larger city's amenities. While statistics indicated a growing town with high-paying technology jobs, Riverside remained a community with little civic engagement, few amenities, and a stubbornly high crime rate.

The Town of Port City

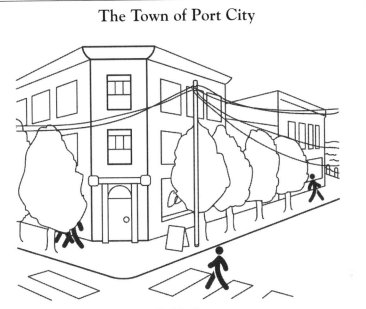

Figure 2.4 Port City has a Walkable Downtown

Port City's history is tied to the maritime industry. Founded over two centuries ago as a mercantile seaport, the city has enjoyed a fairly steady but slow-growing economy. With the help of the state, the city was able to adapt to changing technologies and convert to a small containerized cargo port. The work done by hundreds of stevedores in years past is now done by a handful of crane and equipment operators. While these skilled jobs offer high salaries, many blue-collar jobs in the city's warehouse and distribution industry offer lower pay. Some residents argue that the town needs to attract companies with high-er-skilled jobs, but the common response to this is "these warehouse jobs were good enough for my parents, so they are good enough for me." Port City is a town of modest homes, but civic and social bonds developed over many years remain strong. Recreational sports are important to Port City residents, and the city has an extensive park system to support them. Neighborhood associations are strong and encourage the involvement of residents in civic affairs (Figure 2.4).

Because of relatively lower incomes for most households and fewer wealthy residents, there are not many outward signs of economic prosperity in Port City. Retail stores sell modestly priced merchandise and restaurants serve family-style meals. Except for a small maritime museum and gift shop, there are no galleries, concert halls, or other arts-related venues. However, the city does encourage outdoor seasonal arts and crafts fairs and folk concerts that attract people from surrounding communities to enjoy the scenic old port area, purchase the work of local artisans, and eat in local restaurants.

Would the additional information from the visits to Riverside and Port City change how you would rate the prosperity of these two communities? Which one would you prefer to live in? Numerous surveys and studies have cast light on what people like about communities, and they can help us arrive at a more complete definition of community prosperity.

How Do People Rate Communities?

Urban studies expert Richard Florida has examined the factors that influence how survey respondents rate their communities.[3] The factors most closely correlated with high community ratings in his study are shown (in the order of strength of correlation) in Figure 2.5. The results were generally similar for urban and suburban residents but with some differences in the factor rankings.

1. Personal safety
2. High-quality parks and recreation
3. Availability of good-paying jobs
4. Air quality
5. Availlability high-quality arts,
   culture and nightlife
6. Income

Figure 2.5 Survey: Community factors preferred by residents

---

[3] Bloomberg.com, *Bloomberg*, www.bloomberg.com/news/articles/2014-09-19/what-makes-us-the-happiest-about-the-places-we-live (accessed April 12, 2021).

Researchers at the Penn State University Extension Service have also examined the factors associated with residents' evaluation of their community, and they cite two leading studies.[4] The first study by McMillan and Chavis found that the following four factors consistently emerged in surveys as attributes commonly associated with a good community:[5]

1. Membership: a feeling of being invested in the community; having a right to belong and feel welcome.
2. Influence: a sense that they have some say in community issues and that their viewpoints are respected.
3. Integration and fulfillment of needs: the belief that a community has numerous opportunities for individual and social fulfillment, including basic needs, recreation, and social interaction.
4. Shared emotional connection: the sense of a shared history or sense of community with quality interactions.

The second study by The Knight Foundation (Soul of the Community Project)[6] identified factors that were most closely correlated with survey respondents' ratings of "community attachment." The top five factors (in order of importance) were:

1. Social offerings;
2. Openness;
3. Aesthetics;
4. Education; and
5. Basic services.

---

[4] Educator, Walt Whitmer Extension. March 31, 2021. "What Makes the 'Good Community'?," *Penn State Extension*, https://extension.psu.edu/what-makes-the-good-community

[5] D.W. McMillan, and D.M. Chavis. February 10, 2006. "Sense of Community: A Definition and Theory," *Wiley Online Library*, John Wiley & Sons, Ltd.

[6] "Soul of the Community," *Knight Foundation*, https://knightfoundation.org/sotc/ (accessed April 12, 2021).

Leadership and the local economy were also mentioned by survey respondents, but they did not rank as highly as the previously mentioned five factors.

Hierarchy of Needs

Richard Florida draws a correspondence between how residents rate their communities and psychologist Abraham Maslow's hierarchy of needs pyramid (Figure 2.6).

At the base of Maslow's pyramid are basic needs—the necessities of life including food and shelter. One level above that is safety and security, without which little can be accomplished and sustained. Further up the pyramid are the higher-order psychological and social needs of belonging, esteem, and self-actualization, which correspond with the survey respondents' emphasis on community involvement in the studies referenced earlier. Maslow includes creative activities in the top tier, which points to the role of factors such as arts and recreation in building prosperous communities.

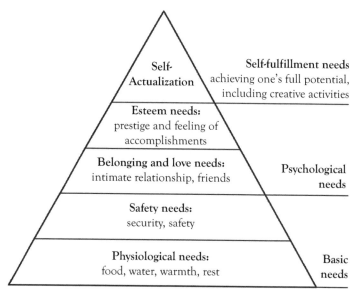

Figure 2.6 Maslow's Hierarchy of Needs

Source: www.simplypsychology.org/maslow.html#gsc.tab=0

Drawing on the surveys and Maslow's hierarchy of needs pyramid, we can group the factors that influence how residents rate their communities into the following four prosperous community components:

1. **Basic Needs** such as safety, public services, and education;
2. **Quality-of-Life Enhancements** such as arts and recreation;
3. **Social Needs** such as feelings of community, involvement, and social fulfillment; and
4. **Economy** including a strong local economic base and good job opportunities for all residents.

Can Money Buy Happiness?

Our discussion of prosperity and happiness leads us to ponder yet again an eternal question: can money buy happiness? Our holistic definition of prosperity might lead us to answer no, but let's consider some different "philosophical" perspectives on this question. Draw your own conclusions and apply as you see fit.

Figure 2.7 Can money buy happiness?

It is a good thing to have money and the things that money can buy, but it's good too, to check up once in a while and make sure you haven't lost the things money can't buy.
— George Horace Lorimer, Editor of the *Saturday Evening Post* from 1899 to 1936.

When will people realize that time, not money, is what really matters?
— Billy Bearden, Former MVP for the All World Softball League

Money doesn't buy happiness. Some people say it's a heck of a down payment, though.
— Denzel Washington, Award-Winning Actor

Money doesn't make you happy. I now have $50 million dollars but was just as happy when I had $48 million.
— Arnold Schwarzenegger, Actor and former governor of California

Sources: "TOP 25 MONEY DOESN'T BUY HAPPINESS QUOTES | A-Z Quotes." 2021. *A-Z Quotes.* www.azquotes.com/quotes/topics/money-doesn't-buy-happiness.html
Billy Bearden quote from Robert Pittman, coauthor (Figure 2.7).

Building on a Strong Local Economy

While not explicitly considered in Maslow's pyramid, jobs and incomes are necessary to provide for human needs at all levels. Food, shelter, and other basic needs do not materialize out of thin air, except perhaps from the replicator on the starship *Enterprise* in Star Trek. A strong economy also helps provide opportunities for meeting human needs higher up Maslow's pyramid such as creativity and accomplishment, which are related to the prosperous community components of Quality-of-Life Enhancements and Social Needs. Arts activities are often supported by a combination of public and private funding. Profitable companies and well-paid employees help support the arts through patronage and contributions. A healthy economy also leads to higher tax revenues that can provide public support of the arts through grants and other forms of assistance. In addition, financially prosperous communities are often more capable of supporting community improvement organizations such as the United Way that provide opportunities for citizen involvement and personal fulfillment.

These connections between a strong economy and prosperous community components help explain why the McMillan and Chavis study cited previously concluded that:

> Evidence suggests that businesses and residents place considerable importance on community characteristics that go far beyond simply a vibrant economy. Importantly for many communities, a strong social and aesthetic foundation is critically important to building a healthy and sustainable economy ....

In other words, just as a strong economy helps support desirable community characteristics, the latter also supports the former—it is a two-way street.

While locally-owned businesses may be more committed to staying in their hometowns, location decisions for larger companies with multiple facilities can be quite complex. They seek communities that offer reasonable operating costs and opportunities for favorable profit margins. They typically compare and screen communities on basic operational factors such as labor cost and quality, transportation services and costs, and the availability and price of land and buildings.[7] However, for business and personal reasons, after meeting these basic operational requirements, most business owners and managers would naturally prefer to locate in a community offering a desirable quality of life, good educational resources, and a strong sense of civic commitment. In addition, with the pandemic-related emphasis on remote work discussed in Chapter 1, many knowledge workers are freer to move to amenity-rich communities that meet

---

[7] R.H. Pittman. 2012. "Location, Location, Location," *Management Quarterly*, https://doi.org/10.4324/9780203049556

their social preferences. In turn, these skilled workers make the communities more attractive to businesses. This helps explain the conclusion from the Knight Foundation study cited earlier that communities with the highest levels of "community attachment" also had the highest economic growth rates.

How Does Your Local Economy Measure Up?

Financial analysts use many different metrics to gauge the performance and outlook for companies. They know that current performance is not necessarily an indication of future performance—overall economic trends, product demand, and competition can change quickly. Likewise, executives monitor their firm's performance and external conditions regularly to look for early warning signs that could affect profitability or even their continued viability.

In a similar fashion, communities should monitor their economic performance to maintain and enhance their prosperity. As several examples in this book attest, the sudden closing of a major employer can devastate a community overnight. While not as dramatic, the gradual decline of major industries and other job-providers in a community can have the same effect over time. As with companies, current performance is no guarantee for the future performance and prosperity of communities. Here are some ways communities can monitor their economic strength and vulnerability:

- Track key economic indicators such as the unemployment rate, personal income, and income per capita. Be aware of trends in these measures—up or down—and investigate their causes. Of course, much of the variation in these key indicators can be closely linked to national trends and this has to be factored into any assessment.
- Benchmark these economic indicators against other communities, your state and the nation to see how your community stacks up currently and also to spot trends.
- Track the performance of the industries in your community. Make a list of industries sorted by employment in the

community. Data to do this are available from a number of sources such as the U.S. Department of Commerce and U.S. Department of Labor. How are the major industries in your community performing at the national or international level? Are they growing or declining? This will provide clues to the future performance of your local economy and need for diversification or even rebooting.

- Monitor your local economy from the ground up. Stay in touch with employers in your community to see if they are growing or declining. Most employers appreciate a visit from a local economic development professional or volunteer. Confidential surveys can add to the information gained through visits and direct contact.

Complacency can be dangerous. Smooth economic sailing today may mask turbulent waters ahead. Smart communities, like companies, watch for signs of danger—and opportunity—and plan accordingly. For more information on monitoring and measuring your community, see Phillips and Pittman, Chapter 21.[8]

A Tale of Three Cities

Riverside and Port City are different communities with their own individual set of strengths and weaknesses. Riverside, with its high-tech jobs, rates highly in the economy component but falls short in some aspects of the other three prosperous community components of basic needs (high crime rate), quality-of-life enhancements (limited support for local retail and restaurants), and social needs (limited community involvement). Port City is almost a mirror image of Riverside, scoring well in basic needs (safety) and quality-of-life enhancements (arts and music festivals) but lower in the economy category than Port City with its high-tech jobs.

So, which town would most people consider more prosperous and prefer to live in? The answer, of course, depends on individual preferences.

---

[8] R. Phillips, and R.H. Pittman. 2015. *An Introduction To Community Development*, New York, N.Y: Routledge.

People who emphasize economic opportunities might prefer Riverside even with a high crime rate and lack of social interaction, while others might prefer Port City because it meets their desire for community involvement. As the saying goes, people are free to "vote with their feet" and seek communities that match their preferences. Other people seek to shape their communities to match their preferences and definition of prosperity—and that is a central focus of community and economic development.

We have discussed how a strong economy can help a community achieve the social characteristics that residents desire, which in turn can help build an even stronger economy. It appears that Riverside and Port City have not yet realized this synergy. Now let's bring a third contender into our community comparison. The city of Overton profiled in the accompanying box has managed to reboot its local economy twice to achieve higher levels of economic prosperity and build a community rich in the characteristics that residents prefer, including quality-of-life enhancements and the social needs of belonging and involvement. No community is perfect and Overton will always face challenges and issues, but it has demonstrated that it knows how to adapt, reboot, and prosper.

Figure 2.8 Welcome to Overton

Overton (Figure 2.8) is a survivor. It has transformed itself and rebooted its economy at least twice before, meeting the challenges (and opportunities) from national and global economic trends. Like countless communities in rural areas, Overton started out as an agriculture market town serving the business and personal needs of local farm families. The postwar economic boom and shift to the production of consumer goods provided an opportunity that Overton embraced. Local leaders knew that Overton's farm families were hard working and resourceful. When the combine breaks down in the middle of a harvest, farmers find a way to fix it and get the job done. Not only were residents extremely productive and resourceful, their cost of living was also lower and wage scales more competitive than their counterparts in higher-cost urban areas. Overton saw a way to capitalize on the labor force asset and strengthen its economy; so, with help from the state government, it developed programs and incentives to entice manufacturing firms to relocate there and enhance their competitiveness with a more productive labor force.

New manufacturing jobs with higher incomes fostered growth in other sectors in Overton, including retail, home building, education, and health care, thus creating a stronger and more diversified local economy and more personal wealth. Change is constant, however, and years later Overton's manufacturers began to move offshore looking for the very thing that helped build Overton's economy—lower labor costs. Overton's leaders realized that communities now had to compete in the world of advanced manufacturing requiring higher-skilled labor operating sophisticated production equipment.

Fortunately, economic prosperity had helped build strong civic bonds, and the community pulled together to reboot again. They realized that education and training programs, as well as new industrial sites and buildings, were needed to attract modern advanced manufacturing firms, so Overton built a regional coalition with surrounding communities. They worked together to create an advanced manufacturing curriculum at the community college serving the area and developed a regional industrial park that attracted a large international company with high-paying jobs. Thus, for the second time, Overton succeeded in rebooting its economy, this time in conjunction with surrounding communities in a true regional effort.

The Tale of Three Cities illustrates our point that community prosperity has many dimensions. Based on numerous surveys and studies on how residents rate their communities, prosperity is more than just economic success. Riverside achieved economic success but did not translate that into quality-of-life enhancements and community involvement. On the other hand, Port City had a more cohesive community but less economic progress. Overton, however, was able to achieve true prosperity with a strong economy, quality-of-life enhancements, and social needs through citizen involvement. Recreational boaters sometimes use the phrase getting up "on plane." Many modern boats start out plowing the water like older wooden boats, but as they gain speed, they come up on plane, guiding on the surface for greater speed and maneuverability. We can say that Overton has come up on the plane of community prosperity and is ready to face the future confidently.

A Roadmap to Community Prosperity

Let's dig a little deeper into the four components listed previously that constitute our definition of community prosperity. Figure 2.9 lists some major factors or characteristics under each component that contribute to community prosperity. The list is not comprehensive, nor is it tailored to a specific community. A principle of community and economic development is to build a community that meets the priorities and vision of its residents, not one that meets a generic checklist. Therefore, to apply Figure 2.9 to your particular community, it should be customized to include prioritized factors that are more highly valued by your community and omit or minimize factors that are not highly valued. For example, residents of a suburban community might desire more close-to-home retail shopping and restaurant options yet be content with driving to the adjacent metro area for arts and entertainment.

Each factor can be further defined in more detail. Infrastructure can include transportation, public utilities, and telecommunications, and those categories can be further subdivided. For example, transportation infrastructure can include highways, roads, airports, public transportation, and so on. For a large city airport facilities and public transportation might be a priority, but for a small town local roads might be the focus.

A large city might want to improve its higher education offerings, while a small town might limit its focus to K-12 education. Customizing and prioritizing the community components and factors should be accomplished by following the community development processes of gathering broad input, making inclusive group decisions, and creating a shared vision for the future. If resources were unlimited, any community could shoot for the moon and pursue excellence in all of the factors, but in the real world, budget constraints prevail. Creating a shared vision helps a community decide what components and factors to focus on and set budget priorities.

Prosperous Community Components	
Basic Needs	**Social Needs**

• Safety
• Public services
• Education
• Infrastructure
• Environmental quality and safety
• Housing
• Health care
   (Customize for your community)
	• Membership
	• Influence
	• Integration and fulfillment of needs
	• Shared emotional connection
	• Openness—welcoming and inclusive
	   (Customize for your community)

Quality-of-Life Enhancements	**Economy**

• Recreation
• Arts
• Entertainment
• Retail/Restaurants
• Neatness/Attractiveness
• Access to community amenities
   (Customize for your community)
	• Strong employment base
	• Diversification
	• Quality jobs
	• Economic opportunity for all residents
	   (Customize for your community)

Figure 2.9 Prosperous Community Components

Now let's put these community components and factors together to create a roadmap for community prosperity. Figure 2.10 shows the four components surrounding and supporting a prosperous community.

The ring road and interior roads shown in Figure 2.10 illustrate the connectivity among the four prosperous community components. We have discussed the numerous connections between the economy and the other components a strong economy generates: income and tax revenues to support basic needs, such as public safety, and quality-of-life factors

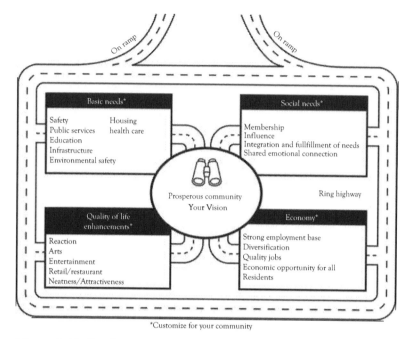

*Customize for your community

Figure 2.10 Roadmap to community prosperity

such as retail and restaurants. The economy and social needs components are also interconnected as the Knight Foundation study referenced earlier concluded.

The Roadmap as a Decision Tool

Ring roads have on-ramps, and in Figure 2.10, they illustrate a useful aspect of the prosperous community roadmap—a filter or tool to help make important strategic and budgeting decisions. To understand this, let's look at two examples. First, consider a community whose local privately-owned hospital is experiencing financial difficulties and is requesting public-sector support. Elected officials in the community could make that decision themselves, or they could create a citizens task force to study the issue and offer options and recommendations. The task force could include representatives from the local medical community, bankers or others with financial expertise, and perhaps marketing experts to suggest ways to generate more revenue. This approach would directly address the basic need of health care but also relate to the social needs component by increasing citizen involvement and influence. Residents might feel more comfortable with the decision to support or not support the hospital with public funds knowing that a group of their peers with the appropriate expertise had input into the decision.

In addition, the economic impact of the hospital should be considered. Hospitals bring money into the local economy through insurance payments and payments from patients in the larger regional hospital market. This money supports health care jobs, and those employees spend money in the local economy on housing, food, and numerous other consumer goods. The question of whether to financially assist the hospital, therefore, should be evaluated on how it affects all prosperous community components, not just the basic need of health care.

As a second example, consider a community embroiled in a heated debate over developing a highway by-pass. Some residents might support the by-pass to help alleviate traffic congestion, while others, especially in-town merchants, might be opposed because of the potential negative effect on existing businesses. At first blush, the by-pass might be viewed as a transportation and quality-of-life issue with some potential effect on local businesses; however, there could also be larger economic issues at stake. The by-pass could open up access to land favorable for industrial development, making the community more attractive to new businesses looking for good sites and good transportation access. It could lead to overall economic growth that could benefit existing local businesses and encourage new ones to open.

These examples illustrate how the prosperity roadmap can assist communities in making decisions. Issues such as a highway by-pass or supporting the local hospital generally affect a community in many different ways along the ring road, and these interactions among the prosperous community components should be taken into consideration.

There is a second important decision-making element underlying these examples. When deciding on matters such as the by-pass or support for the hospital, consideration should be given to how a community wants to grow and develop—its vision for the future (see accompanying box). In the case of the by-pass, does the community want to grow more quickly and attract new businesses and chain retailers along the by-pass, or would it prefer to remain a tourist destination with a quaint downtown retail district? Community residents opposed to the by-pass might argue that it will create noise and pollution, while those in favor might argue that it will relieve traffic congestion. These are certainly valid issues, but chances are an underlying bone of contention is different visions for the community.

Community Visioning

"What do you want to be when you grow up?" is a question mothers, fathers, aunts, and uncles often ask children in their families. This question has prompted countless young minds to think about what their future might be—or what they can make it be. Many companies also think about what they aspire to be when they "grow up," and become bigger and better organizations. Here are some examples of company mission statements or visions:

IKEA: "To create a better everyday life for the many people."
Nike: "To bring inspiration and innovation to every athlete in the world."
Tesla: "To accelerate the world's transition to sustainable energy."

A vision can help keep an organization's employees focused on a shared purpose and promote teamwork. Studies have shown that employees who believe in their organization's vision statement are more engaged than those who do not.

A vision statement can have a similar positive benefit for a community working to move forward and achieve prosperity. A community vision statement can be brief, reflecting general values such as—Columbia, Missouri's "Columbia will be a connected, informed and engaged community" or it can be more detailed like these excerpts from the vision statement of Lakewood, Colorado:

We envision a community that is a great place to live; a community that cares about the environment, and a community that maintains a high quality of development.

We envision a growing and diverse business sector that provides residents with a wide range of products and competitive services.

There are proven procedures a community can use when creating a vision in order for it to be motivating and successful. A process of developing the vision should be inclusive, giving everyone in the community a chance to express their opinion on the community's future. The vision statement must be realistic, but at the same time be challenging to inspire the community to work hard to achieve it. More information on community vision statements is in Chapter 3's discussion of the community development process.

Sources:

R. Phillips, and R.H. Pittman. 2015. *An Introduction To Community Development*. New York, N.Y.: Routledge.

"22 Vision Statement Examples To Help You Write Your Own | Brex," 2021. *Brex.Com*, www.brex.com/blog/vision-statement-examples/

"Community Vision—Master Plan | The City Of Lakewood, Ohio," 2021. *Lakewoodoh.Gov*, www.lakewoodoh.gov/community-vision/

Now let's mix the roadmap to prosperity together with visioning and planning to create a comprehensive community decision-making and budgeting tool. Elected officials can be bombarded with requests to fund this or that cause or project. Individually, they can be worthwhile; and if they are not funded, their proponents often proclaim: "How could you *not* fund this wonderful project?" The problem is that there are many worthwhile projects but limited budgets. Too often, political connections and lobbying determine budget priorities with little thought to synergies and long-term community benefits. Just as well-run companies make investment decisions based on returns—how they will contribute to profitability and the company's mission—communities should make budget decisions based on how they contribute to prosperity. Here are three steps to accomplish this:

1. *Create a vision and plan for the community* as outlined in the accompanying box and discussed in Chapter 3.

2. *Use the vision and plan to customize and prioritize the prosperous community components and factors list in Figure 2.9.* As an example, consider a town named Bridgecreek with the vision to become the leading upscale tourist destination in the state by attracting tourists with fine dining restaurants, art galleries, and recreational amenities. To facilitate this vision Bridgecreek could prioritize quality-of-life factors, such as neatness/attractiveness, and basic needs, such as environmental protection and public safety.

3. *Use the customized list of prosperous community factors as a filter to help make strategic and budget decisions.* In Bridgecreek, a plan to create a streetscape with enhanced off-site parking in the downtown area would be a higher budget priority rather than a developer's request for incentives to build an amusement park. Interactions among the prosperous community components as discussed earlier should also enter into Bridgecreek's budget decisions. A more attractive downtown with sidewalk cafes and other amenities could entice more local residents to congregate there, increasing social interaction and reinforcing the sense of community.

Using a community's vision and customized prosperity roadmap lends openness and transparency to the public decision-making and budgeting process. To make a point, the authors sometimes ask elected officials if they have ever gotten undisputed unanimous support for a first budget draft. The answers range from incredulous looks to howls of laughter. Community residents and stakeholders disagree on budget priorities for many reasons, but as discussed previously, they often do so because they have different visions for the future of the community. The simple question "does this proposed expenditure help us achieve our community's vision?" can make life much simpler for elected officials.

Getting the Mayor Off the Budget Hot Seat

During a break in a seminar taught by the authors, the mayor of a small town close to a metro area told the author that he had to prepare his first draft budget, and it could make or break his young political career. He explained that the town was divided between residents who wanted to build a youth sports complex and those who wanted to develop a speculative industrial building to attract companies, and the town did not have the budget to do both. We told him there was a relatively simple way to answer that question to help get him off the hot seat. We suggested that he first engage the community in a visioning and planning exercise to address, among other issues, if the consensus was to: (1) remain a bedroom community with residents continuing to commute to the metro area, or (2) attract more businesses to the town and give residents options to work locally, and to diversify and expand the town's tax digest. If the consensus was the latter, then it would make more sense to start the economic development process and develop the building to help attract a company to the town. He thanked us profusely and said, "Now I can say I'm carrying out the will of the people," to which we replied, "Shouldn't all budget decisions be based on that?"

Newly elected officials sometimes complain to us that the pressure to take positions on issues during the campaign and after taking office often forces them to make decisions too quickly without adequate knowledge or public input. Occasionally we read about newly appointed CEOs spending their first weeks on the job talking to as many people in the organization as they can before making any decisions. Perhaps decision making in many places could be improved if elected officials would start their time in office the same way to help the community achieve its definition of prosperity.

A Journey or a Destination?

Now that we have explored its many dimensions, we can offer a more concise working definition of community prosperity:

A prosperous community is one that maintains a strong and diversified local economy to provide economic opportunity for all residents, provides for the basic needs of residents, offers quality-of-life enhancements preferred by residents, and meets the social needs of residents through community involvement.

You may think that your community meets this definition, or you may believe it falls short. No community is perfect, and there will always be differences of opinion on how any community measures up and on where there is room for improvement. In this light, we should think of community prosperity as a journey rather than a final destination. Circumstances are always changing—communities will face economic shocks such as the loss of major employers, and "new normals" will bring challenges and opportunities. Communities must adapt and even reboot in response to changing circumstances as Overton did in our Tale of Three Cities.

To make our definition of community prosperity more dynamic, we could add to it the ability to adapt to changing internal or external circumstances to sustain prosperity. Even a gold medal-winning athlete must train for the next Olympic event at a new venue with new competitors. Just as a gold-medalist celebrates his or her tremendous accomplishment while preparing for the next competition, communities should celebrate their achievements and milestones but continue their efforts to become even more prosperous. Now that we have a working definition of community prosperity and understand its underlying components, the question becomes how to attain it and sustain it—how to get up and remain "on plane" like a sleek speedboat. That is the focus of the remaining chapters.

Prosperous Community Toolbox

Read, Reflect, Share, and Act

Chapter 2 challenges us to think about the definition and level of prosperity in our own communities. Prosperity means different things to different people, however experience has shown that by using community development tools a consensus definition of prosperity and a commonly-shared vision for a community can usually be reached. This chapter offers tools that can help your community build its own definition of prosperity.

The Chapter 2 tools will help your community create a first draft of your roadmap to prosperity with input from all who call your community home, and to create a tracking system to measure your community's prosperity.

2.1 Create a prosperous community website to help gather survey responses in 2.2 below and from the community visioning exercises in Chapter 3 and other public input, and to keep residents informed of community prosperity efforts and programs.

2.2 Based on extensive community input, identify and prioritize the community components and factors that residents believe best define your community's prosperity. In other words, create a first draft of the prosperous community components and factors table such as Figure 2.9 for your community. Look for common elements in all the community feedback and comments as input for developing a vision and plan for the future of the community (Chapter 3 toolbox). Revise and finalize the prosperous community components table after completing a community visioning exercise in Chapter 3.

2.3 Create a spreadsheet or other model to assess and track the strength of your community's economy in the ways suggested in the box "How Does Your Community Measure Up" in this chapter. Find a suitable local person or persons (committee) to build, operate and update the model and issue reports to the local officials and the public. Decide on the measures to be tracked (economic, demographic, social well-being and other desired measures). Identify and report trends in key measures, positive or negative. This will be an integral part of the visioning exercise in Chapter 3.

Visit https://www.prosperousplaces.org/rebooteconomics_toolbox/ to download worksheets and templates for the Chapter 2 tools.

The Real Overton

The example of Overton in the Tale of Three Cities is based on the real-life community of Tupelo and Lee County, Mississippi. Tupelo's success in applying community and economic development best practices to achieve prosperity and reboot has been extensively chronicled in articles and books. Much of the prosperity in Tupelo and Lee County has come about through regular and comprehensive community visioning, goal setting, and planning. The city and county believe in establishing a foundation for prosperity through the community development process, and then building on that with the economic development process—the subjects of Chapters 3 and 4. A regional foundation for community development called CREATE was established decades ago to encourage strategic planning and collaboration around shared goals. Tupelo's vision and plan for prosperity centers around the following six themes:

1. Orderly, efficient land-use patterns;
2. Economic vitality;
3. Neighborhood protection, revitalization, and housing opportunities;
4. High-quality design and development;
5. Efficient and accessible transportation; and
6. Regional coordination.

Tupelo and Lee County have utilized the tools in the toolbox to embrace and benefit from change and achieve sustainable prosperity. As a result, Tupelo has been named an "All American City" five times by the National City League.

Sources:

V.L. Grisham, and R. Gurwitt. 1999. "Hand In Hand," Washington, D.C.: Aspen Institute, Rural Economic Policy Program.

Author discussions with Tupelo/Lee County officials.

CHAPTER 3

Laying the Foundation

A Prosperous-Ready Community

January 2013: The downtown was relatively empty, with a few antique stores hanging on along with several law offices near City Hall. The area had been prosperous once, bustling as a regional center with the railroad running right through town. The downtown, surrounded by hundreds of historic homes from the early 1900s, was like so many other small to mid-sized towns throughout rural America—a shell of its former self. Fast forward five years and this town became a media darling and tourist destination. How did this happen and what prompted this rather dramatic makeover within such a short timeframe?

The answer lies in … community development! Laying the foundation is the starting point for responding to opportunities (even those no one could see coming) and creating opportunities for paths forward to prosperity. This is what community development is all about—building a strong foundation on existing assets and working to improve conditions and opportunities. To find out more about this turn-around story, see more details and the reveal at the end of this chapter. But before you skip to the end, let's discuss some "bricks-and-mortar" fundamentals of laying a solid foundation for a prosperous-ready community.

This chapter shows how the process of community development, including creating a vision and addressing community issues through an inclusive strategy, paves the way to the outcome of a prosperous-ready community. This solid foundation then provides the basis for the process and outcome of economic development, increasing the flow of money into the community, thus creating new jobs and higher incomes. And it's about more than just money, because by engaging in community development, social cohesiveness (sometimes called social capital) and other desirable community aspects and assets are strengthened. All these elements, or "capitals" of a community, are ingredients for the recipe of place making or creating community prosperity. A beautiful wedding cake is an artful blend of layers and icing. Community development creates the layers, and economic development provides the icing of economic opportunity for all residents.

The field of community development has expanded greatly in recent years as researchers and practitioners have learned more and developed even better roadmaps to community prosperity. The same is true for economic development. Our goal in Chapters 3 and 4 is to outline the basics of community and economic development and identify some tools to help communities practice them with greater success. Detailed information about the theory and practice of community and economic development can be found in the chapter notes and references.

The Fundamentals of Community Development

Community development is both a practice and a field of study. Towns, cities, regions, and states practice it, and numerous universities and organizations offer degree and training programs for elected officials, citizens, and others interested in improving their communities. It is founded on the premise that a city, town, or neighborhood is more than just a collection of buildings; each one is a community of people facing common problems and a desire to improve situations or outcomes. It is about a process—developing the *ability* to act in a positive manner for improvement—and it is about outcomes too. The latter involves taking *action* for community improvement to generate desirable results.

There are many strategies and tools for community development including organization and leadership development, visioning, planning, and mapping assets in the community. There are also many proven "best practice" principles in community development such as ensuring public participation with broad representation from all members of the community, monitoring progress, and making adjustments in response to challenges that may arise. The Community Development Society, the oldest professional and scholarly association in the field, provides the following Principles of Good Practice:[1]

- Promote active and representative participation toward enabling all community members to meaningfully influence the decisions that affect their lives.
- Engage community members in learning about and understanding community issues, and the economic, social, environmental, political, psychological, and other impacts associated with alternative courses of action.
- Incorporate the diverse interests and cultures of the community in the community development process; and disengage from support of any effort that is likely to adversely affect the disadvantaged members of a community.
- Work actively to enhance the leadership capacity of community members, leaders, and groups within the community.
- Be open to using the full range of action strategies to work toward the long-term sustainability and well-being of the community.

You can see quickly from this list that community development is about more than the individual; it is about all members of the community working together for progress.

There are also professional ethical standards in the practice of community development. The Community Development Council offers the following values to guide Certified Professional Community and Economic Development (PCED) practitioners:[2]

- Honesty
- Loyalty
- Fairness

---

[1] "Principles of Good Practice—Community Development Society," 2021. *Comm-Dev.Org*. www.comm-dev.org/about/principles-of-good-practice

[2] "Professional Community & Economic Developer," 2021. *Cdcouncil.Com*. www.cdcouncil.com/PCED.htm

- Courage
- Caring
- Respect
- Tolerance
- Duty
- Lifelong learning

Community development focuses on helping residents understand how economic, social, environmental, political, and other factors influence their community. This knowledge can then be transformed into results through coordinated actions for progress. Community development is about much more than social service programs or bricks-and-mortar construction projects. Instead, it is a "comprehensive initiative to improve all aspects of a community: human infrastructure, social infrastructure, economic infrastructure, and physical infrastructure."[3] It is these dimensions of community development that are important for everyone involved in the process to know, and we recommend that when starting a community development process or plan, you share these principles and values with participants.

Being There for Your Community Makes a Difference

Two key success factors in community development are: (1) the belief that something positive can happen and (2) working together and collaboratively to make it so. These are accomplished by being engaged and participating in your community's place making, or "place keeping" if, for example, you are preserving historic, cultural, or natural assets in a historic district or conservation trust to retain open space. Belief is a powerful force and typically begins when an individual or group of people begin to realize that they can contribute to maintaining or improving the quality of life in their community. Although places can change because of just one person's actions, community development is best performed

---

[3] R. Phillips and R.H. Pittman. 2015. *An Introduction To Community Development*, New York, NY: Routledge.

as a group activity, with strategies emerging from the decision of a group of people to take action. It requires community wide initiatives, which in turn requires collaboration. The context of community development is broad and inclusive, as it literally endeavors to affect the entire realm of a place. Another way of thinking about community development is to think of it as *community building*, including building the foundation of a prosperous-ready community.

Let's discuss for a moment the notion of hope. It's an intangible element, yet it can exert a dramatic influence on a place, as can its opposite, hopelessness, as indicated in the following example. The authors recently worked with two communities about the same size (population under 50,000) with similar histories of development as railroad and agricultural towns. For sake of discussion, we'll call them Sunrise and Sunset (Figure 3.1).

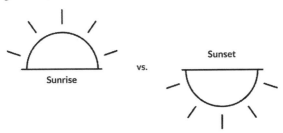

Figure 3.1 Some communities are sunrise and some are sunset

Both communities have experienced various states of economic decline since the 1970s and 1980s when agriculture transitioned to a larger-scale industrial focus and small industries (such as assembly and components parts manufacturing or textiles) left the United States for Mexico or overseas.[4]

Sunrise is now doing very well in economic and social terms and enjoying prosperity. Residents have aspirations and developed plans

---

[4] There are quite a few studies, books and other writings about changes in rural America. For example, look at resources from the U.S. Department of Agriculture or any of the Rural Regional Development Centers. If you're in the mood for a story about this instead, see the essay "Community Development and Economic Development: What is the Relationship? " by R. Phillips (2016) and Sharpe, Erin K, Heather Mair, and Felice Yuen. n.d. *Community Development.*

that reflect their hopes and dreams for their community. They've built on their assets, which include a significant palette of historic properties from the early 1900s, and they are committed to preserving their historic districts ensuring that absentee owners maintain properties. Not many deteriorating structures in Sunrise! The local government maintains the park system and common areas and decorates for holidays and festivals. By maintaining aesthetically pleasing visuals, they create an environment that is interesting and attractive to others—a strong sense of place. In some ways, they were lucky. Their historic downtown was frozen in time because not much development had occurred for decades, so when they were ready to start revitalizing, the raw material on which to do so was waiting, mostly intact.

Sunset similarly has a varied and deep fabric of historic properties and a parks system designed in the early 1900s during the City Beautiful Movement era. The city was once an attractive destination on the rail line in a bygone era. But, here is what greeted us when we arrived: litter strewn everywhere, graffiti (but not the artistic type like found in some Detroit neighborhoods now on the graffiti trail attracting viewers, tourists, and artists) and dilapidated structures throughout the city. The widespread situation very clearly signaled a lack of any policy enforcement for absentee owners to maintain properties. Envision vines growing over derelict buildings, sometimes right next to well-maintained properties. This kind of blight depresses property values and deters others from investing in the community. Public areas were not maintained, and parks and crumbling infrastructure needed attention. To its credit, Sunset had invested in a new rail station and preserved part of the historic building, but it was quite evident that numerous historic structures had been lost. The charred remains of one historic downtown building serve as a constant reminder to residents and visitors of forever-lost assets.

What makes the difference in these two cities? It's hard to know the whole story without further investigation of these places, but one thing very clearly emerged. When asked why they embarked on their community development journey, Sunrise stakeholders responded with "because we care about each other." Likewise, we asked Sunset stakeholders why they had not started community development efforts and the response was "because no one cares." In fact, they stated that a sense of hopelessness pervaded the community, and many who may have once been interested in taking actions "have lost hope" or left. With these examples, you can see what the presence of caring and hope can do for a place. It doesn't mean that attitudes can never change, but it does show that how residents feel about their community and each other can heavily influence community development and prosperity.

Hope, caring, and a sense of shared responsibility—these attitudes influence the willingness of a community to take actions and move forward. It really isn't enough to *wait for something to happen*, it's up to residents and stakeholders *to make it happen*, literally. This is the essence of community development.

Being Ready for Development

A big part of community development and laying the foundation for successful economic development is identifying and nurturing assets in the community. What are community assets? Simply put, they are resources, skills, talents, and experiences inherent within a community's individuals, organizations, and institutions. Assets also include the stock of monetary wealth of households, organizations, and local governments. There are several types of assets that are considered in community development including human, social, financial, environmental, cultural, political, and physical.[5] The stock or level of these assets in a community can be referred to as community capital. Financial assets are critical for supporting community development efforts as shown in the roadmap to prosperity in Chapter 2. Infrastructure, as part of physical capital, is essential for supporting physical development. Also important to community development is achieving a balance between the cultural and political elements or capitals of a community so that a sense of shared purpose can overcome differences and challenges. Experience clearly shows that groups of residents working together toward shared goals generates more desirable community development outcomes. Over 2000 years ago, Aristotle recognized this too, stating that the goal is not about following the rules, but about performing

---

[5] Green and Haines. 2007. *Asset Building and Community Development.* Thousand Oaks, CA: Sage.

social practices well. Certainly, community development is a social practice and needs to be performed well to be effective! Each of the community capitals can be further subdivided; for example, physical capital can include natural resources as well as the built environment.

While all of the community capitals are important, two are often pre-eminent: human and social capital. Let's define them in more detail to see why. Haines describes human capital as:

> ... the skills, talents, and knowledge of community members. It is important to recognize that not only are adults' part of the human capital equation but children and youth also contribute. It can include labor market skills, leadership skills, general education background, artistic development and appreciation, health and other skills and experiences. In contrast to physical capital, human capital is mobile. People move in and out of communities, and thus over time, human capital can change. In addition, skills, talents and knowledge change due to many kinds of cultural, societal, and institutional mechanisms.[6]

Another community asset or capital that is vital to community success is social capital. It would be difficult if not impossible to have much success in community and economic development without some degree of this type of capital asset. It can be defined *as the extent to which members of a community can work together effectively*[7] to develop and sustain strong relationships; solve problems and make group decisions; and collaborate effectively to plan, set goals, and get things done.[8] Social capital is often divided into two types: bonding capital among similar groups and bridging capital among different groups. The more social capital a community

[6] A. Haines. 2015. "Asset-Based Community Development," In *Introduction to Community Development*, eds. R. Phillips, and R. Pittman. 2nd ed., 45–56. London: Routledge.

[7] P. Mattiessich. 2015. "Social Capital and Community Building," In *Introduction to Community Development*, eds. R. Phillips, and R. Pittman. 2nd ed., 57–73. London: Routledge.

[8] R. Phillips, and R. Pittman. 2015. "A Framework for Community and Economic Development," In *Introduction to Community Development*, 2nd ed. London: Routledge.

has, the better it can meet challenges and work around deficiencies in the other types of capital.

Human capital and social capital are different from the other capitals because they describe the abilities of community residents to work together and get things done. It's apparent that human capital—the abilities and assets of individuals in the community such as leadership and education—is critically important for building prosperous communities. Success would surely be limited if, for example, residents of a community had no leadership skills. As we've discussed, groups of people working together effectively drive the community development process, and social capital describes the ability of residents to do that.

Political capital, like human and social capital, is intangible but also very important in the process of community development. Political capital has been described as "a metaphor used in political theory to conceptualize the accumulation of resources and power built through relationships, trust, goodwill, and influence between politicians or parties and other stakeholders, such as constituents."[9] Trust, goodwill, and other aspects of political capital are obviously related to human and social capital.

These three closely related intangible community assets: human, social, and political capitals, can be considered the "software" or human components of the community development process. The other capitals mentioned earlier—financial, environmental, cultural, and physical—are the "hardware" of community development. They are the hard or tangible assets that residents use to create community prosperity as programmed by the software.

How does a community increase its stock of social capital? This is done through the process of capacity building, which is designed to strengthen the problem-solving resources of a community.[10] Capacity building can be done through activities such as community and neighborhood organizing, developing formal and informal institutions and organizations, and collaborating toward shared goals.

---

[9] U. Kjaer. 2013. "Local Political Leadership: The Art of Circulating Political Capital," *Local Government Studies* 39, no. 2, pp. 253–272. doi:10.1080/03003 930.2012.751022

[10] P. Mattiessich. 2015. "Social Capital and Community Building," In *Introduction to Community Development*, R. Phillips and R. Pittman. 2nd ed, 57–73. London: Routledge.

The Community Development Chain

Simply put, the community development *process* includes two components: (1) taking action to improve the community and (2) developing or enhancing the ability to take action. The process then leads to the *outcome* of community development—a great place to live, work, and play. But a positive outcome of community development also supports the process—it is a two-way street as illustrated in Figure 3.2 and described as follows:

> The solid lines show the primary flow of causality (from process to outcome). However, there is a feedback loop shown by the dotted lines. Progress in the outcome of community development …. contributes to capacity building (the process of community development) and social capital. For example, better infrastructure (e.g., public transportation, internet access, etc.) facilitates public interaction, communications and group meetings. Individuals who are materially, socially, and psychologically better off are likely to have more time to spend on community issues because they spend less time meeting basic human and family needs. Success begets success in community development; when local citizens see positive results (outcomes), they generally get more enthused and plow more energy into the process because they see the payoff.[11]

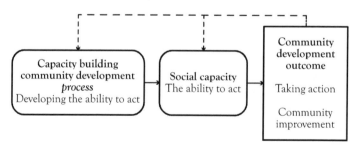

Figure 3.2 The community development chain

---

[11] R. Phillips and R. Pittman. 2015. "A Framework for Community and Economic Development," In *Introduction to Community Development*, 2nd ed, 9. London: Routledge.

The community development process can influence the type as well as amount of growth experienced within a community. Prosperous places create their own futures through effective application of the community development process that empowers residents and other stakeholders to change in desired directions—to follow their own roadmaps to prosperity. Development should be goal-oriented, and not change for the sake of change. Community development is based on the foundational principle that residents and other stakeholders have the capability (or can develop it) and responsibility to undertake community-directed initiatives for the good of all residents.

Creating a Community Vision

Once a community understands its assets including the important dimension of social capital, then it's time to start the visioning process. The biblical adage that those without a vision will perish applies to community development. Communities without a vision may not be destroyed by a plague of locusts, but they are at a greater risk of growth and development happening "to" them instead of "for" them as noted earlier in the book. Understanding your community's assets is an important place to start because it helps create a realistic and attainable vision. When a community's vision is coupled with the process of community development and action, good things start to happen. The Orton Family Foundation, a nonprofit organization, believes that "empowering people to shape the future of their communities will improve local decision making, create a shared sense of belonging, and ultimately strengthen the social, cultural and economic vibrancy of each place."[12] They developed the *Heart & Soul Community Planning* handbook focusing on helping communities actualize this mission in their own places. The organization states, "Vision without action is a dream. Action without vision is simply passing the time. Action with Vision is making a positive difference." Vision is a guide to making a community what it wants to be, and that is why vision is at the center of the roadmap to prosperity in Chapter 2.

---

[12] Programs, Our, FIRST League, FIRST Challenge, FIRST Competition, FIRST Fair, GIRLS' GEN, and Summer Opportunities Alumni et al. 2021. "ORTOP," *ORTOP*, https://ortop.org/

Why just wish for the future to happen to your community? Prosperous communities know that the future is something they can direct and create based on what they want to achieve. Community visioning is therefore an essential element of community development. The process itself can be just as important as the output as it brings together all residents and stakeholders from within a community to discuss ideas, identify challenges and opportunities for improving overall well-being and quality of life.

There are many guidebooks and other resources on the visioning process, some of which are listed in the Toolbox at the end of this chapter. Here, we will share some basic guidelines that have proven effective in numerous community visioning projects across the United States. These guidelines focus on collaboration and consensus building that are vital to the visioning process. Without broad-based participation, getting support and buy-in from others in the community is difficult to do. Community visioning is different and more inclusive than some of the downstream community and economic development efforts such as identifying prospects for an industrial park. Here are the guidelines that can make for a successful community visioning process:

- People with varied interests and perspectives participate throughout the entire process and contribute to the final outcomes, lending credibility to the results.
- Traditional "power brokers" treat other participants as peers.
- Individual agendas and baggage are set aside so that the focus remains on common issues and goals.
- Strong leadership comes from all sectors and interests.
- All participants take personal responsibility for the process and its outcomes.
- The group produces detailed recommendations specifying responsible parties, timelines, and costs.
- Individuals break down racial, economic, and sector barriers and develop effective working relationships based on trust, understanding, and respect.
- Participants expect difficulty at certain points and realize it is a natural part of the process. When these frustrating times

arise, they step up their commitment and work harder to overcome these barriers.

- Projects are well timed—they are launched when the time is right for making it happen.
- Participants take the time to learn from past efforts (both successful and unsuccessful) and apply that learning to subsequent efforts.
- The group uses consensus to reach desired outcomes.[13]

After completing the visioning process, communities should develop a strategic plan to attain their vision with goals and action items attached to each goal. In other words, visioning should not just identify wonderful items that are desirable in the community; it should also include realistic goals and action items with assigned responsibility for them. The visioning process should include financial and other resources for each goal in as much detail as practicable. Evaluation and reporting should be included in the visioning and implementation processes using a format agreeable to the community. It is important to know how much progress is being made toward the vision goals so that recalibrations can be made as needed. Sometimes, the goals may change as conditions do—just imagine how many community and business goals have changed due to the pandemic. Since uncertainty is a certainty, it is important to adjust goals and actions in response to unanticipated developments while keeping the community vision firmly in sight as the target. Completing a visioning process and developing an implementation plan will create a foundation for subsequent growth and development and help a community achieve its definition of prosperity.

Being Creative in Development Approaches

Recall the four main components of a prosperous community in Chapter 2 and the factors or characteristics under each one. Three of the main

---

[13] M. McGrath. 2015. "Community Visioning and Strategic Planning," In *Introduction to Community Development*, eds. R. Phillips and R. Pittman, 2nd ed., 125–126. London: Routledge.

components—basic needs, quality-of-life enhancements, and social needs—are directly aligned with community development. The fourth component, the economy, relates more directly to economic development. However, as discussed in Chapter 2, the four components reinforce each other and therefore the processes and outcomes of both community and economic development are key ingredients for community prosperity. Community development creates a "prosperous-ready" foundation and economic development draws on this to create jobs, investment, and income. But, the world is constantly changing and creating "new normal" situations, so in this section we want to look at some new ways of thinking about how to build a solid foundation for prosperity. While considering these examples, keep in mind that there are many other creative ways to support development such as sports venues and activities as well as strategies for encouraging tourism to draw in visitors and more money into the community. We just can't cover them all here.

Arts-Based Development

As we've discussed previously in the book, quality-of-life enhancements, depending on community preferences, often include arts and culture. These are also related to the other prosperous community components and can be used to spur creative ways to accomplish community and economic development. Cities and towns around the globe have found that the arts can play a crucial role in local development efforts. The amenities and aesthetics of a place can enhance its overall image and consequently help attract additional development. Some places, including small towns such as Jerome, Arizona or Toppenish, Washington, treat the whole town as an art object with murals and artists venues. Larger places such as Duluth, Minnesota focus on rejuvenating the arts and other quality-of-life factors as part of a larger development strategy. Duluth is a great example of integrating the arts into community development planning and strategy (see the following box). Public art becomes a way to strengthen and define a place. Such is the case of Loveland, Colorado where hundreds of sculptures create a park-like environment in the city and make art a major attraction. This concentration of public art helped attract related companies and activities to Loveland, including specialty arts, bronze casting, and other arts-related enterprises. Silicon Valley may have its cluster of technology companies, but Loveland has created its own cluster of arts-related activities and businesses.

Returning Prosperity to Duluth, Minnesota

Duluth, MN

Figure 3.3 Duluth, Minnesota

Duluth, located on the western end of Lake Superior, developed as a major port for shipping iron ore to steel mills along the Great Lakes and agriculture products from mid-western states to markets in the United States and abroad. During the 1970s and 1980s, Duluth experienced a number of economic shocks, including the decline of the U.S. steel industry and competition from other ports. A steel production facility located there closed in 1979, leaving 5,000 people unemployed and a contaminated site. Unemployment in Duluth peaked at nearly 20 percent in the early 1980s, by which time the population had declined by over 20 percent from a peak of over 106,000 people in 1960. Tax revenues declined as economic stagnation continued. In 2008, the city faced a $4.4 million budget deficit, and in 2009 Moody's issued a negative outlook for the city's bond rating. National industry trends were not kind to Duluth, and the city fell from prosperity.

Duluth clearly needed to reboot its economy and reboot it did. Building on its location as a gateway to the scenic beauty and recreational opportunities along the northern shore of Lake Superior, the city took steps to enhance its appeal to younger residents by promoting music festivals, the arts, and outdoor recreation including hiking and biking trails. Without turning its back on its industrial heritage, Duluth rebranded itself as a genuine "battle-tested" city where entrepreneurs can grow their businesses while enjoying nature, culture, and a more relaxed lifestyle.

The commitment to enhance and market the quality of life in Duluth paid off, and both homegrown and relocating businesses expanded in the city. Maurice's, a clothing retailer with hundreds of stores in the United States and Canada, built an 11-story headquarters building in downtown Duluth. Homegrown companies such as Loll Designs, maker of outdoor furniture, and Epicurean, maker of cutting boards and other wooden kitchen products, expanded there. While the local taconite mining industry continued to operate in the region, other industries including health care, education, and tourism as well as the above-mentioned companies grew and helped create a stronger and more diversified local economy. The city has proven that it can handle diversity and emerge on the other side even stronger.

Duluth is a great example of a forward-thinking "can-do" community that rebooted its economy and followed the roadmap to prosperity. It also illustrates the interconnection between the community components of quality of life and the economy. In this case, the economic recovery was stimulated by the city's proactive strategy of investing in the arts, recreation, and other amenities, creating a new image or brand as a great place to live and build a business.

Sources:

"Turnaround Towns". 2021. *Carnegie UK Trust.* www.carnegieuktrust. org.uk/project/turnaround-towns/

"Innovative Duluth | Twin Cities Business". 2021. *Twin Cities Business.* https://tcbmag.com/innovative-duluth/

Performing arts can also serve as a catalyst for community and economic development. Music can attract visitors by the thousands to places such as New Orleans with its Jazz and Heritage Festival and North

Carolina with its Merlefest. Visitors are also attracted to smaller towns to celebrate regional musical styles. Examples include Eunice, Louisiana with its Cajun music, and Mountain View, Arkansas with folk music. Both are now major tourist attractions. Performing arts also include theater, movies, and television. Colquitt, Georgia profiled in the Introduction, rebooted its local economy through innovation in performing arts with its *Swamp Gravy* production.

Some communities market themselves as a location for film or television productions. Many communities offer natural beauty, historic treasures, or built environments that provide backdrops for filming. Most states have a film office to promote their communities for filming, and it can be a big business in places such as Savannah, Georgia or Las Vegas, Nevada. But, it's not only the larger places that can benefit. Dyersville, Iowa, where *Field of Dreams* was filmed, has a population of only 3,500, but the filming created the basis for continued tourism. Thanks to the smart strategy of the local Chamber of Commerce to buy merchandising rights to the movie, *Field of Dreams* made decades ago keeps tourist dollars flowing to Dyersville businesses. Likewise, Bozeman, Montana is widely known as the site for the film, *A River Runs Through It*. The town attracts tourists because of the movie and the related industry of sport fishing.

Building Prosperity With Community Enterprises

Not all places have natural beauty or tourism potential like the examples above, but what every place does have is the ability to consider community-owned enterprises as an option. These types of enterprises touch on many of the prosperous community components, including the social, quality-of-life, and economy components by encouraging members of the community to work together for economic progress. Community-owned businesses are just what they sound like: investors (usually residents) pool together resources to buy or build an enterprise that is needed or desired. This approach can be taken in response to the closing of a grocery store, restaurant, retail store, or even a local pub (England has quite a few pubs that are community-owned).

Community Capitalism?

Community-owned enterprises often arise when there are no other options to keep essential services or to encourage the kind of development a community prefers. Several places in Montana and Wyoming have community-owned stores because there can be large distances between towns and no easy way to commute for shopping elsewhere. Some places are turning to community enterprises to address situations detrimental to public health and well-being, such as the lack of access to fresh food sources. For example, in St. Paul, Kansas the local government now owns and operates the community's grocery store.[14]

Community-owned businesses are growing in popularity, and they are a new twist to an old institution (cooperatives) that can run the gamut from agriculture to buyer membership groups. They can also be formed for industrial production. Such is the case in the region of Emilia-Romagna in Italy where 30 percent of the gross regional product emanates from cooperatives. In fact, Emilia-Romagna has the largest concentration of cooperatives in the world. The Basque region in Spain is home to the largest single cooperative in the world, the Mondragon Corporation, a worker-owned enterprise. The cooperative movement is coming full circle. Cooperatives were once very popular in the earlier part of the 20th century, and now they are returning, creating locally focused enterprises to help build prosperous communities. Host communities often tout the virtues of cooperatives as ways to keep revenue, investments, and quality jobs in the local economy. Think creatively! If an opportunity exists in your community, a community-owned enterprise may be a viable option.

Historic Attractions as a Community Development Strategy

Many places have a rich and varied array of historic structures. Sometimes, these structures are at risk of being lost while at the same time there may be unmet demand for housing or other needs in the community. Why

---

[14] N. Walzer. 2021. *Community Owned Businesses*, 1st ed. Routledge.

not think out of the box and consider establishing a community trust for acquiring suitable historic properties to rehab as affordable housing or even for use as public spaces? While community trusts often take the form of organizations for conservation of natural areas or preservation of farmlands, there is growing interest in establishing trusts for acquiring historic structures. This is a situation where collaboration and partnership building may be needed to acquire funds for acquisition. At the same time, housing is the one of the largest uses of land in most cities and towns so there could be significant potential to increase the supply, opportunity, and affordability of housing. Perhaps you are aware of renovations of historic houses or buildings in your community that helped spur nearby improvements. Renovated historic structures can serve as a catalyst and inspire more development projects. Even a few renovated houses on a street can change things rapidly; community developers call this the "window box effect."

We are connected to our built environments deeply and improving historic assets so that community members can see progress helps further develop that ever important "sense of place." We should never underestimate its importance. Sense of place is sometimes hard to define, but we know it when we experience it. Think of a charming downtown, seaside village, or iconic New England town that you've visited. Chances are it was graced by historical buildings. We normally don't describe our communities in terms of ubiquitous fast food joints or strip malls even though they serve important functions. Instead, we tend to describe them in terms of their unique features including historic homes and structures such as a courthouse of Indiana limestone or a railroad hotel from a bygone era. Your community may even have a theater built long ago in need of restoration. Renovating old theaters or similar structures can serve as a catalyst for bringing together people to focus on their community. Why is this? Because old theaters back in their day were places to gather and experience a sense of community.

There are many places where historic preservation efforts stimulated development and attracted other investments into the community. Examples include Cape May, New Jersey's Victorian seaside resort, and Eureka Springs, Arkansas' Victorian village in the Ozark Mountains. Historic preservation can serve a vital role in community development, cutting across basic needs (infrastructure and housing), social needs (shared emotional connection), quality-of-life enhancements (arts and entertainment), and the economy from an increase in tourism. For an example of the broad impact historic preservation can have on a community, check out the story behind the renovation of a long defunct textile mill into the Mass MoCa center in North Adams, Massachusetts and the benefits accruing to the community and region.[15]

The Rebirth of a GEM: A Personal Reflection

Long before big screen TVs with video streaming and home surround sound systems came into vogue, there was a time when movie theaters were a social focal point for many small towns across America. Families attended theaters to be entertained and see places around the world they had only dreamt about. As a child growing up in Newnan, Georgia, 25 cents would buy me a Saturday morning of western and sci-fi adventure with my friends at the Alamo Theater. For another quarter or two, I could eat my fill of popcorn and candy.

When I was a teenager, my family moved to Calhoun, Georgia, and the Martin Theater became my new Alamo. James Bond and *Rosemary's Baby* replaced cowboys and radioactive aliens but going to the movies (maybe even with a date!) was still a social event. Like many rural communities, Calhoun's downtown lost its vibrancy to a neon strip of new discount stores and fast food restaurants just outside of town. The Martin Theater [previously known as the GEM theater (Figure 3.4) founded in 1927 as Calhoun's only arts and movie venue] left downtown and built a new triple screen cinema where its customers were now shopping and dining.

With philanthropic help from a local family, a group of citizens formed a nonprofit corporation to save a piece of Calhoun's history and restore the GEM to its former glory and role in the community.

---

[15] Tickets, Get, Plan Visit, FAQ Info, Courtesy Code, More Museum, Sound Art, and LeWitt S. et al. 2021. "MASS Moca," *MASS Moca | Massachusetts Museum of Contemporary Art*, https://massmoca.org

With money raised from public and private contributors, the renovated GEM Theater reopened in 2011, once again providing the residents of Calhoun and Gordon County with an opportunity to get together downtown for dinner and a show, and perhaps some shared memories of cinematic days gone by. From the GEM's website:

> *The GEM features the best of both the past and present, as its appearance takes you back to 1939 and its amenities provide a state-of-the-art theater experience. The original GEM is best remembered as a movie theater, but the renovated 461-seat GEM showcases a variety of entertainment including concerts, plays, and movies ... After more than 70 years, the GEM has finally come full circle to entertain the citizens of Calhoun in all its original beauty and elegance .... Most importantly, the GEM is the community's theater. It is the 'gem' in Calhoun's crown.*
> *Source:* https://calhoungemtheatre.org/about/

—Robert Pittman

GEM / Martin Theatre

Figure 3.4 GEM/Martin Theatre

Historic preservation and creating a sense of community can also make a town more attractive to remote workers and companies in the new geography of work described in Chapter 2. This is just one example of community and economic development opportunities in the post pandemic new normal.

Well-Being and Sustainability

As mentioned earlier, measuring and tracking change is necessary to assess how a community is progressing, and what strategies and actions are working better than others. More specifically, communities should focus on measuring the community components and factors they have set as top priorities. However, some desired attributes and goals for a community cut across the four main components in our model of community prosperity. For example, health care was classified in Chapter 2 as a basic need without specifying its extent or quality because that is normally a function of community size. You wouldn't expect a world-class cardiac care facility in a small town, but you would expect (or hope for) primary health services such as emergency treatment or hospitalization for common illnesses. In larger communities, you could expect secondary care from specialists. In even larger metro areas, you would expect tertiary care, such as heart bypass surgery, or even services such as experimental treatments that are classified as quaternary care.

However, some communities might want to set the bar higher for health care because of an older or vulnerable population, or simply because it is a community priority for all residents. The National Rural Health Association has given top ratings to 20 rural hospitals in places such as Brookings, South Dakota; Monroe, Wisconsin; and Pratt, Kansas.[16] Going above the norm and achieving higher standards for services such as health care or education usually requires special efforts including the development and utilization of stronger ties among the four prosperous community components. Outstanding health care facilities don't usually

---

[16] "Top 20 Rural Community Hospitals—NRHA," 2021. *Ruralhealthweb. Org*, www.ruralhealthweb.org/about-nrha/rural-health-awards/top-20-rural-community-hospitals

just spring from a community's desire to provide basic services. Involvement and commitment to the community (social needs) and strong financial resources (economy) also play a role in most cases.

The concept of well-being is getting increasing attention in the field of community development. Dictionary.com defines well-being as "a good or satisfactory condition of existence; a state characterized by health, happiness, and prosperity." This is consistent with our definition of community prosperity in Chapter 2 based on the four components of basic needs, quality of life, social needs, and the economy. However, the concept of well-being cuts across these four components and offers an even higher-order meaning of community prosperity.

In practice, most definitions of well-being in a community development context focus on the physical and emotional health of residents; some also include other things such as how well people meet their social needs, including interacting with each other in community decision-making processes. Various surveys and reports indicate that social bonding is a very important factor influencing well-being. Hence, there can be synergy here: community involvement by itself can improve community well-being, but it can also contribute to better community services such as health care. Whether measured by specific indicators or overall assessments, "being well" has taken on even more significance in the pandemic era.

Communities can and should have their own definitions of well-being depending on their priorities. For example, Lafayette, Indiana created their "Good to Great" plan in 2012 focusing on quality-of-life dimensions that influence their definition of community well-being. Since then, they have developed more biking trails and encouraged healthier, local food choices. Each year the community gathers data on quality of life to help focus efforts and revise them as needed.[17] Places such as Lafayette that include measures of well-being in their planning and development activities will be more in tune with how their community is progressing on the road to prosperity.

---

[17] "Quality of Life—Greater Lafayette commerce," 2021. Greater Lafayette Commerce, www.greaterlafayettecommerce.com/quality-of-life/

Well-being is very closely tied to community sustainability, which is often divided into social, economic, and environmental sustainability as noted in a publication from McGill University:

> Sustainability means meeting our own needs without compromising the ability of future generations to meet their own needs. In addition to natural resources, we also need social and economic resources. Sustainability is not just environmentalism. Embedded in most definitions of sustainability, we also find concerns for social equity and economic development. Without sustainability, the well-being of future generations is compromised.[18]

The prosperous community components provide a useful framework for understanding and implementing sustainable policies. Numerous surveys such as those cited in Chapter 2 show that community residents rank environmental safety as a very high priority. Places not providing the basic needs of clean air and water are not prosperous-ready. Contrary to the beliefs of many people, studies have shown that a strong economy can actually contribute to sustainability by making people less likely to sacrifice tomorrow's resources for today's economic growth.[19]

Realizing the importance of sustainability to community prosperity and well-being, many communities are beginning to incorporate sustainability into their community and economic development planning. Chattanooga, Tennessee, and Burlington, Vermont, are taking this approach; the smaller town of Truckee Meadows, Nevada is taking a regional approach to sustainability. Attention to sustainability and well-being can encourage a community to focus on its needs and assets for attaining prosperity. Connecting well-being, sustainability and community development can yield positive outcomes.

---

[18] 2021. *Mcgill.Ca*, www.mcgill.ca/sustainability/files/sustainability/what-is-sustainability.pdf

[19] "Why Economic Growth Is Good for the Environment," 2021. *PERC*, www.perc.org/2004/07/01/why-economic-growth-is-good-for-the-environment/

The Bridge to Economic Development

Creating a prosperous community, like building a house, involves two phases: (1) laying the foundation of a "prosperous-ready" community and (2) building on that foundation with economic development to achieve prosperity. Without that solid foundation, economic development efforts will most likely yield disappointing results. We do not wish that result for your community, so we strongly encourage you to build the foundation of a prosperous-ready community that is attractive to businesses, entrepreneurs, tourists (if that is part of your vision and plan), and residents who want a high quality of life and social opportunities. Understanding and applying the principles and practices of good community development will start you on your journey to community prosperity and building a place where residents enjoy the things that matter the most to them.

Prosperous Community Toolbox

Read, Reflect, Share, and Act

Chapter 3 of *Rebooting Local Economies* is about what you need to do to create a path to a more prosperous community so that you can start responding to and creating opportunities of your own. Establishing a strong foundation is essential for making use of your current assets, as well as identifying ways to improve your current condition (whatever it may be), and seizing opportunities.

Chapter 3's tools are designed to help you identify the assets and resources your community already has that can make it more prosperous, measure your community's social capital, and gain feedback from your community to understand your current situation.

3.1 Map the assets in your community. Conduct an asset mapping exercise or survey to find assets that can make your community more prosperous. Sometimes these are apparent and sometimes they are hidden (for example, skill sets that may exist across a group of residents). Asset mapping affords a better understanding of the relationships and synergies among a community's assets.

3.2 Gauge your community's social capital. Learn the characteristics of successful communities and community builders through the chapter's worksheets and use those guides to rate your community

3.3 Take the Civic Index. The National Civic League developed the Civic Index to help communities measure and develop skills and processes for evaluating and improving their civic infrastructures. This index can aid the community visioning process and planning and strengthen problem-solving capacity.[20]

3.4 Get feedback on your community. Ask colleagues, friends, or others who visit your community to comment on what they see, both positive and negative. This is just another way of gathering objective input for your strategic plan for community and economic development. Work to build on the positive while remedying the negative.

3.5 Start a community visioning process. This is a significant undertaking, but as discussed in Chapters 2 and 3, it is quite essential for designing your community's roadmap to prosperity. Use your draft roadmap from Chapter 2 and the above tools in Chapter 3 as inputs to the visioning process. After you have completed the process, revisit the draft Roadmap to Prosperity in Chapter 2 and adjust as appropriate. Visit www.prosperousplaces.org/rebooteconomics_toolbox/ to download templates and guides for the Chapter 3 tools.

---

[20] "Civic Index- 4th Edition," 2021. *National Civic League*, www.national civicleague.org/resources/civicindex

How to Become a Media Darling or the Case of Creating Opportunity

Figure 3.5 Laurel, MS

Who would have ever thought a town of 18,000 in the Piney Hills region of Mississippi would become a tourist destination? That's exactly what has happened since the renovation show, *Home Town*, started airing on the HGTV network. It's about more than renovating houses like so many other shows. It includes a healthy measure of community development; the couple hosting it declares that they want to help revitalize their home town of Laurel (Figure 3.5). In the five years since the show began, Laurel has seen noticeable change due to new businesses dedicated to making over numerous homes and historic buildings in the town.

Interest in living in Laurel has noticeably increased. People from California, Arizona, and many other states have moved to the town's historic districts with oak-lined streets and bordered by a parks system designed by none other than Frederick Law Olmstead in the 1800s. Laurel, known as the City Beautiful, has long been noted for its charming downtown and historic structures, as well as the short train ride on the historic Crescent Line to New Orleans. The train station has been renovated to preserve its historic charm. In the past, streetcars traversed the city built around the timber industry.

What made the difference, or should we say who made the difference? Young millennials started renovating historic structures downtown for upper floor condominiums and flats, drawing in people to live downtown. This led to the establishment of the Main Street Program that spurred further interest in the historic downtown and adjacent neighborhood districts. New businesses moved in, helping create an environment of locally focused enterprise imparting a unique feel and strong sense of place.

When hosts Ben and Erin Napier returned to Laurel after college, they decided to invest their artistic and building knowledge into renovating properties. When postings on social media caught the attention of a production company, they were asked to create a pilot, and the rest is history. Laurel became a sensation overnight, and while not every community will be lucky enough to have a television show produced in their town, the success speaks to how prepared the community was when opportunity came knocking. Laurel's success also illustrates the mindset of creating opportunity—making things happen by building on the assets in a community. All places have them, but sometimes they are not evident. In the case of Laurel, the historic buildings were sitting there, waiting for opportunity. Community members and leaders in Laurel had the mindset to take advantage of the town's assets and were ready to act when opportunity came. Being ready to take advantage of opportunity is an essential principle of community development; it prepares the community for positive economic development outcomes.

CHAPTER 4

Building a Prosperous Community

"We almost hit the point of no return," the mayor of Osceola, Arkansas told *The Wall Street Journal* in 2006. Like many rural communities, Osceola, a town of about 7,000 in Northeast Arkansas' Mississippi County, grew up around the agriculture industry. As farm employment declined, textile-manufacturing jobs grew but ultimately disappeared as the industry moved offshore. In 2001 Fruit of the Loom shut down its Osceola plant leaving 2,500 people unemployed and the community in a crisis. Not only was unemployment rampant, the school system was classified as academically distressed and faced a state takeover. But what a difference a few years and an all-out community effort can make! Today Osceola has a strong economy supported by successful companies such as Japanese auto parts manufacturer Denso and Big River Steel with its $1.3 billion technologically advanced flat-rolled steel plant employing over 600 people. How did Osceola and Mississippi County reboot the local economy? You can skip to the end of the chapter for the rest of the story, but we encourage you to read the chapter first to fully appreciate this example of community resilience.

As discussed in Chapter 3 and illustrated by numerous examples throughout the book, how well a community engages in the commu-nity development process can be a key determinant of its community development outcomes. This includes strengthening the four community components on the roadmap to prosperity: basic needs, quality of life, social needs, and the economy. The community development process can improve the provision of basic needs such as public safety and education, and enhance the quality of life through citizen involvement, advocacy, and financial support. The cornerstone of the community development process is involvement and leadership, thus helping residents meet their social needs and feel more attached to the community. But, how does the community development process contribute to the fourth prosperous community component, the local economy? This question is the primary focus of this chapter and a central theme of the book.

You Want a Prosperous Community? Show Me the Money!

When Liza Minnelli sang, "Money Makes the World Go Round" in the 1972 movie *Cabaret*, she coined a phrase that persists to this day and provides a basic lesson in economics (if only we could all learn economics through song!). Money and its equivalents are the lifeblood of commerce, and it does make the economic world go round. Let's start with the premise that more money is better than less. On a personal level, more income coming in than going out would make us feel more prosperous. Personal cash flow can vary considerably in the short run due to things such as such as getting a bonus or buying a car, but over the long run if cash flow is positive, then wealth is growing.

This is also the case with inflows and outflows of money at the community level. Local residents, businesses, and other stakeholders in a community have their own net inflows or outflows of money, and the sum of all those can be considered the community's cash flow. If it is positive, the level of total wealth in the community rises as illustrated in the accompanying box. Money enters the community through businesses selling their goods and services to outside consumers, direct payments to residents from out-of-town sources, and in miscellaneous other ways. Money leaves the community when businesses pay out-of-town suppliers and shareholders, and residents spend money outside of the community shopping and vacationing.

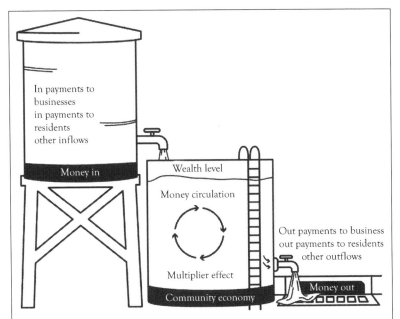

Figure 4.1 Community money flow and wealth

Figure 4.1 is a simple model of money flow and wealth for a community. The level of water in the tank represents total community wealth. Water (money) flowing into the tank raises the level of wealth, and water flowing out of the tank lowers it.

Money flows into the community tank from these sources:

- **In Payments to Businesses**: Local businesses sell goods and services to buyers outside the community, receive payment, and then pay employees and local suppliers. Businesses involved in tourism and hospitality are included in this category. When tourists visit, they spend money in restaurants, hotels, retail stores, and other places. Businesses and other organizations (e.g., nonprofits) that bring outside money into the local economy are often referred to as export businesses. It's important to note that in this context, export means anywhere outside of the community, not necessarily out of the country. Businesses that sell goods and services, mainly to community residents, can be referred to as local market businesses. For example, a hardware store selling mainly to community residents in a small town would be considered a local market business, whereas a Home Depot that pulls in customers and money from surrounding communities would be considered an export business.

- **In Payments to Residents**: Residents receive money from numerous outside sources such as retirement payments, investment income, and now increasingly from employers outside the area for residents engaged in remote work.
- **Other Money In**: Federal or state government installations and offices, nonprofits, and other miscellaneous organizations receive money from outside sources. Note that *local* government facilities and operations do not typically increase the water level very much in the tank. Local governments are more cash flow neutral because the money they spend in the local economy mainly comes from the local money they take out of it through taxes.[1]

Money flows out of the community tank through these sources:

- **Out Payments by Businesses**: Local businesses purchase raw materials and intermediate goods as well as services from outside suppliers to produce their own products and services.
- **Out Payments by Residents**: Residents make payments to outside sources when they shop online or in surrounding

[1] Local government spending can, however, have a net positive effect on the local economy in at least two ways. First, local governments may purchase fewer outside and more local goods and services than residents would have with the money paid in taxes. Second, some of the money paid in taxes would likely have been put in savings by local residents, and the local government "saving rate" may be lower (and therefore the consumption rate higher) than that of the taxpayers.

towns, eat in nonlocal restaurants, take vacations, pay tuition for out-of-town colleges, and a host of other activities.

- **Other Money Out**: Local governments and other local organizations purchase goods and services from out-of-town providers. Residents and businesses pay taxes to federal and state governments.

As Figure 4.1 also portrays, money circulates inside the community as businesses, residents, and governments sell and purchase goods and services to and from local sources. This gives rise to the economic multiplier effect. Let's say, for example, that a local manufacturing company lands a large new out-of-town customer and hires 100 unemployed workers to increase production. These 100 new workers will then purchase more local goods and services with their increased income (buy a car, eat out more often, or maybe even buy a house). This income that is recirculated within the community, in turn, stimulates additional local employment and income to satisfy the increased demand, and then the cycle repeats itself.[2]

The community cash flow model in Figure 4.1 illustrates two simple but important concepts for community prosperity:

1. **Positive cash flow**. If a community's cash flow is positive over time (money in exceeds money out), the water level in the tank rises, and total wealth increases. If wealth increases faster than the population, then per capita wealth grows.
2. **Keep money in the community**. Keeping money circulating in the local economy and not going out keeps water in the tank and increases community wealth.

These two simple concepts help explain many of the economic development activities undertaken by communities:

[2] H. Galloway. "Understanding Local Economies." in R. Phillips, and R.H. Pittman. 2015. *An Introduction To Community Development*, New York, N.Y: Routledge.

- More businesses in a community selling their products and services to customers outside of the area bring in more money to support more local jobs and incomes. More inflow and jobs can be created by recruiting new businesses into the community, helping local businesses expand, and stimulating new business startups. The same applies to governments or organizations in the "Other In" category.
- Outside payments coming into residents also support local jobs and incomes because recipients spend some of it locally. Some communities promote themselves as a good place to retire for this reason.
- Reducing outside payments by local businesses helps keep money in the local economy and increases total wealth. Programs to encourage more local sourcing of raw materials and intermediate goods can help. The same applies to government or other organizations included in "Other Out."
- Reducing outside payments by residents also keeps money in the local economy. This is the philosophy behind "buy local" campaigns by chambers of commerce and economic development agencies.

In the movie *Cabaret*, how much did the Kit Kat Klub contribute to local economic development and community prosperity in 1920s Berlin? We do know that out-of-town patrons would have contributed to the community's money in flow, and if the club procured its supplies locally, that would help keep money circulating in the local economy. Beyond that, we can only speculate on the club's impact on the local economy (maybe more jobs for police?) and on other prosperous community components such as the quality of life. We leave that to the reader's judgment.

Economic Development as an Outcome

When a new company selling to out-of-town customers begins operations in a community, when an existing company expands or tourism increases, more money flows into the community creating more jobs. This puts cash in people's pockets to buy groceries, clothes, haircuts, and countless other goods and services in the community, thereby creating even more jobs through the economic multiplier effect. As businesses continue to expand and more jobs are created outward signs of prosperity begin to appear—more industrial, commercial and retail buildings, more houses, and more restaurants. These are the outcomes of economic development. However, as the accompanying box explains, economic development can mean different things to different people and different communities, reminding us of the observation in Chapter 2 that economic development can either happen "to you" or "for you." Taking the proactive approach of defining and pursuing preferred economic development outcomes helps communities avoid the "to you" and encourage the "for you."

Is It Economic Development or Just Growth?

"We don't need economic development, we need jobs!" proclaimed a small-town mayor over refreshments following a training session led by the authors. (Note for file: provide stronger libations at future seminars.) Actually, the mayor's comment helps us think about what economic development really means. Perhaps, the mayor was thinking about some of his lower-skilled constituents—we can't all be rocket scientists. He might view economic development as something that involves skilled workers in larger cities with new subdivisions, retail centers, and stadiums.

Some might say that economic development, like beauty, is in the eyes of the beholder, and there is some truth to that. For some small towns a new fast-food restaurant or dollar store can be a significant event that provides an additional dining or retail option as well as an employment opportunity. Newly hired employees probably wouldn't care if you call it economic development or not—it's still a paycheck to them. Residents of larger communities with bustling economies, however, might look at fast-food restaurants and dollar stores as just more sprawling growth and congestion and more stoplights. In such communities, the bar can be set pretty high. Anything less than a new technology firm with high-paying jobs might not be considered real economic development. Thus, the distinction between economic development and growth can very much depend on one's perspective.

When we say a community is growing, what does that really mean? We can envision situations where growth occurs without meeting a higher standard of economic development, but it is hard to conceive of economic development without growth. More jobs and higher incomes will increase the demand for housing, retail, and personal services. As the authors travel around the country (physically or virtually), we sometimes encounter local officials who want a booming economy without the traffic lights and congestion—the economic development version of having your cake and eating it too. The Southern take on this usually goes something like "we want good jobs, but we don't want to be like Atlanta," a reference to the city's legendary rush hour traffic jams. This is certainly an admirable goal, and perhaps the new normal of remote work is a tentative step in that direction. Remote workers, however, are not hermits—they still get out of the house to shop, dine, get a haircut, or visit friends. Smoothing out the peaks of rush hour traffic will ease congestion considerably, but for the foreseeable future, the main course of economic development with more jobs and higher incomes will continue to come with a side of orange road construction barrels.

Economic Development as a Process

Because we can learn much by example (sometimes referred to as "concept learning" by psychologists), we have included numerous stories of communities that have rebooted and prospered in the book. These communities are diverse in terms of size, location, and circumstances. The one thing they have in common is that, when faced with adversity, they did not simply wait for the next strong wind to push them off the shoals. Instead, they took decisive action to get themselves back on the journey to prosperity. Granted, a shock such as the downsizing or closing of a major employer can be a tremendous motivator, but all across the country and around the world communities are improving themselves simply because they want to do so.

As shown by the community wealth tank illustration in Figure 4.1, there are various ways to increase the flow of money into the local economy and decrease the outflow to create more economic prosperity. The inflow can be public or private money. Some communities are heavily dependent on public money to support the local economy:

- In Vermont's capital of Montpelier, state government employees directly account for 29 percent of the city's workforce and 32 percent of wages paid.[3]
- In Huntsville, Alabama, the Redstone Arsenal, a center for U.S. Department of Defense research and contracting, is estimated to directly and indirectly generate 90,500 jobs and $10.6 billion in economic output.[4]

Some communities are heavily dependent on a local college or university while others are retirement havens with large inflows of public and private pension payments.

Mostly, though, the private sector accounts for the majority of employment and income and constitutes the "backbone" of a local economy. In 2019, the private sector accounted for almost 64 percent of U.S. gross domestic product.[5] In addition, communities generally have more influence in helping create private sector jobs through recruiting new businesses and encouraging new business startups. For these reasons, we

---

[3] 2021. *Montpelier-Vt.Org*, www.montpelier-vt.org/DocumentCenter/View/1223/Economics-and-Livelihoods-PDF

[4] 2021. *Hsvchamber.Org*, http://hsvchamber.org/wp-content/uploads/2017/09/redstone_economic_impact_analysis_may.pdf

[5] Statista. 2021. *United States——Ratio of government expenditure to gross domestic product (GDP) 2026 | Statista*, [online] Available at: <www.statista.com/statistics/268356/ratio-of-government-expenditure-to-gross-domestic-product-gdp-in-the-united-states/> (accessed June 07, 2021).

focus mainly on private sector investment as a way to grow jobs and build prosperous communities.

Defining the Term

Now that we've characterized economic development as both a process and an outcome, let's see how some economic development-related organizations define the term. Years ago, the American Economic Development Council (now merged into the International Economic Development Council) described economic development as:

> The process of creating wealth through the mobilization of human, financial, capital, physical and natural resources to generate marketable goods and services ... and benefit the community through expanding job opportunities and the tax base.[6]

The California Association of Local Economic Developers (CALED) offers a similar definition:

> Economic Development is the creation of wealth from which community benefits are realized. It is more than a jobs program, it's an investment in growing your economy and enhancing the prosperity and quality of life for all residents.[7]

These definitions emphasize the following:

- Creating wealth—not just making rich people richer, but giving everyone a chance to improve their economic situation
- Benefiting the community as a whole through creating opportunities and enhancing the tax base

---

[6] American Economic Development Council. 1984. "Economic Development Today: A Report to the Profession," Schiller Park, Illinois.

[7] G. Sahota. 2021. *Economic Development Basics | CALED*, [online] CALED, Available at: https://caled.org/economic-development-basics/ (accessed June 07, 2021).

- Improving quality of life
- Investing in and mobilizing community resources to grow the local economy
- Affirming that the process of economic development leads to the outcome of economic development

Economic development is not just about jobs,—it's about community prosperity.

Development Economics Versus Economic Development

The term economic development is also used in the context of developing countries:

> Economic development ... is the process whereby simple, low-income national economies are transformed into modern industrial economies.[8]

This important field of study is often referred to as development economics to distinguish it from economic development in industrialized countries. The latter is the subject of this book.

While many of the principles of community and economic development apply to both developed and developing economies, there are significant differences. A student from Niger taking a college course in community and economic development taught by one of the authors dropped by during office hours and lamented that he didn't really understand the economic development part of the course. He said, "In parts of my country where there are no paved roads or infrastructure of any kind, economic development is only a dream; but I now understand better why we must concentrate first on community development."

---

[8] Encyclopedia Britannica. 2021. *Economic development*, [online] Available at: <www.britannica.com/topic/economic-development> (accessed June 07, 2021).

What Attracts Businesses to a Community?

To attract and retain more private sector investment and jobs, communities should understand what factors businesses evaluate when making location decisions and how they make them. As previously noted, retail stores and restaurants can be local market businesses or, when they attract out-of-town customers, export businesses. In some communities, especially those that rely heavily on tourism, the retail sector can be a major industry. However, the retail sector is not our focus here; there are other books and sources of information on retail location decisions. Instead, we focus on businesses that produce goods or services to sell to out-of-town customers (export businesses), thereby increasing the flow of money into the community.

As noted in Chapter 2 most companies naturally prefer communities that offer a good workforce, public infrastructure, educational system, and other factors they need to be profitable and grow. In addition, most business owners and decision makers would also naturally prefer to live in communities with a high quality of life for their own enjoyment and to help them attract and retain the best employees. A web search will turn up dozens of surveys of corporate executives and business location consultants on the factors that are most important to businesses when deciding where to locate or expand company operations. In a recent survey by *Site Selection* magazine, consultants listed the following as the most important location factors in order of priority:[9]

1. Workforce
2. Transportation infrastructure
3. Available sites and buildings
4. State and local tax structure
5. Incentives
6. Utilities
7. Regulatory environment

---

[9] R. Starner. 2021. *Site Selectors Survey: More Than Some Like It Hot | Site Selection Magazine*, [online] Site Selection, Available at: https://siteselection.com/issues/2018/jan/site-selectors-survey-more-than-some-like-it-hot.cfm (accessed June 07, 2021).

8. University and college resources
9. Cost of real estate

Surveys of this nature provide useful insights into how companies evaluate communities when making investment decisions, but they are generic whereas location decisions are unique. The location decision factors for a company looking for a new regional headquarters or other office facility would not be the same as those for a company looking to locate a new manufacturing facility. Workforce and education might be key factors for both, but the headquarters company is more likely to be looking for white-collar workers and higher education resources while the manufacturing company is looking for blue-collar production workers and technical training programs. Some business investment decisions are driven by very specific requirements. For example, food-manufacturing facilities often locate close to where the agricultural products are sourced—the raw materials for these facilities. The location decisions of warehouse and distribution facilities are often driven by logistics models that determine exactly where a new facility should go to fit into a complex distribution network.

Just as businesses in the expansion mode seek communities that meet their needs and help make them more profitable, so do existing businesses. Communities should not take for granted businesses that are already located there. Some recent high-profile moves of companies from California with its higher cost and regulatory burden to the Austin, Texas area, illustrate that local signature companies such as Hewlett-Packard, Oracle, and Tesla can be footloose. According to media reports, Elon Musk, owner of Tesla, announced that he would move his headquarters to Texas or Nevada immediately after local governments refused to let the company reopen its Fremont (California) factory. Elizabeth Edwards, founder of Ohio-based H Venture Partners, stated, "The Silicon Valley exodus is real. It's driven by a number of factors, taxes and the cost of living being two reasons."[10]

---

[10] S. Cao. 2021. *Why Elon Musk And Other Tech Billionaires Are Leaving Silicon Valley For Texas*, [online] Observer, Available at: https://observer.com/2020/12/elon-musk-tech-leaving-silicon-valley-for-texas-billionaires/#:~:text=At%20an%20event%20last%20week,it%20was%20not%20unexpected%20news. (accessed June 07, 2021).

At this point, you might be thinking that this whole business location thing seems pretty complicated and expensive, and asking "Do we have to improve our workforce, infrastructure and education at the same time? Even if we tried that, should we focus on technical training or higher education, highways, or internet service?" The answer to this important question can be found in the following phrase, variations of which have been attributed to people ranging from the Apostle Paul to Harvard Business School guru Michael Porter: "A person can't be all things to all people." Likewise, a community cannot be all things to all businesses. A more practical and successful approach to attracting more business investment is outlined in the following three steps.

1. *Understand your community's strengths and weaknesses and its competitive position.*

Picture a new girl in school, Anna, going to softball practice to try out for the team. When the Coach asks her what position she plays, Anna responds that she can play them all. Needing players, Coach tries her out at shortstop, but Anna misses some grounders. In the next game, Coach lets Anna play outfield but she is no better at catching fly balls. Desperate for a pitcher for the next game, Coach lets Anna pitch, and to her great surprise, she strikes out the other side in the first inning. When Coach asks Anna why she didn't just say that she was a good pitcher and make things easier for both of them, Anna responds, "I didn't know what players you needed, and I wanted to make the team; and besides, I wasn't sure I could pitch that well on a new team." Had Anna been more self-aware and honest with Coach, she could have saved herself some embarrassment and perhaps saved the team some losses.

What "position" can your community play best? Community assessments, as mentioned in Chapters 2 and 3, are critical to answering this question. If your community has an experienced white-collar workforce and strong educational resources, perhaps it could be a good location for a company's regional headquarters. If your community is strategically located on an interstate highway connecting major metro areas, it could be a good location for a distribution facility. If your community has a good inventory of potential or developed industrial sites with good utility services, then it could be a good location for a large-footprint manufacturing plant. But, like our softball player Anna, a community cannot play all positions and be all things to all companies. In our professional careers helping companies with their location decisions, we have received many proposals from communities that are obviously not a good fit for a particular project. This is a waste of resources for all parties involved and certainly does not generate any goodwill for the community.

2. Identify industries that are a good match for your community.
To find their target markets, communities identify industries or economic activities that would be attracted to their assets and not put off by their relative weaknesses. Several years ago, one of the authors helped a new commuter jet company find a location for a large production and test facility. Requests for proposals (RFPs) were sent to the economic development agencies for 18 states that met the initial geographic and weather requirements with specifications on the number of clear flying days and industrial sites close to a general aviation airport. Despite these clear up-front specifications, some unqualified communities still submitted detailed proposals, wasting time and generating no goodwill for themselves.

In addition to being a good locational match, communities should identify industries that are consistent with their vision. For example, a community might aspire to transition from its traditional manufacturing base to more technology-oriented industries. If the community has excellent educational resources and internet service, something like a technical support facility might be a good locational fit. Companies that are a good match for a community can run the gamut from goods and services producers to nonprofit organizations to remote workers. The process of matching communities and industries, sometimes referred to as target industry analysis, is not the same as the often-criticized industrial policy of picking "winning" industries to support with public resources. Instead, it is smart target marketing—the same common sense approach businesses take to identify customers that are more likely to buy their products. Like a company trying to sell meat to vegetarians, a community trying to attract companies for which it has no locational advantage is a waste of resources. There are additional screens such as historical and predicted future growth rates that communities can also use to identify industries and companies that are good targets to pursue. Companies in a growing industry are more likely to look for places to expand than those in a declining industry.

3. Strive to become an even better location for your community's preferred and matching industries.

No community is perfect and no community has unlimited resources. Deciding how to allocate public money over many different community needs and desires is an imperfect democratic process. However, as discussed in Chapter 2, using community development principles, such as obtaining broad input and developing a vision for the future, can help communities maximize the benefits from public expenditures. Deciding on the nature and scale of economic development and the kinds of industries a community desires can also help with community planning and budgeting decisions. For example, if a community wants to attract advanced manufacturing companies, then its priorities should include developing suitable industrial sites and creating relevant technical training programs.

Of course, public budget decisions should not be based solely on economic development. Many other factors included in our roadmap to prosperity such as public safety (basic needs) and recreation (quality of life) should be considered. But, a strong economy can definitely help by generating more tax dollars that communities can use to help address a wide range of budget needs (Figure 4.2).

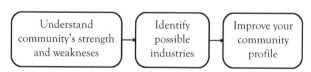

Figure 4.2 Targeting for Economic Development Success

The Economic Development Stool

Through our simple community wealth water tank illustration, we have seen that local businesses selling products and services to out-of-town consumers pipe money into the community, creating jobs and income. The question then becomes how to grow a community's business sector and therefore increase prosperity. This can happen in three basic ways:

1. New businesses moving into the community;
2. Businesses already located in the community expanding;
3. New businesses forming in the community.

These elements can be considered the three legs of the economic development stool (Figure 4.3).

Figure 4.3 The three-legged economic development stool

What can communities do to strengthen these three legs? Some communities take a hands-off approach, reasoning that businesses are naturally attracted to them because they are endowed with the factors that businesses need to succeed such as a good workforce. There are indeed some fortunate communities that are natural magnets for businesses. However, ask anyone in marketing or sales if having a good product is all you need to generate revenues, and you'll probably get answers ranging from "So why are they paying me?" to "Are you nuts? There are lots of good products out there that we compete with every day!"

Hollywood movie lines such as "build it and they will come" notwithstanding, having a good location for operating a business and a good place to live does not necessarily attract investment and generate economic development. As of 2019, there were 19,502 incorporated cities and 3,142 counties in the United States, many of them good "products" competing to attract private or public job-generating investments and grow local businesses through economic development organizations and chambers of commerce. For these communities, the three legs of the economic development stool are often referred to as: (1) business recruitment, (2) business retention and expansion, and (3) new business startups. There are numerous articles, books, websites, and other resources devoted to conducting these three economic development activities. Such detail is beyond our scope in the book, but here is a brief overview of each activity.

1. *Business Recruitment*

Most businesses or organizations, large and small, are dynamic—expanding or contracting depending on their markets and national economic trends. When large national or international businesses are growing and can't expand in existing facilities, they search for new sites or buildings. They can do this with in-house personnel or seek outside assistance, usually business location consultants or industrial/commercial real estate companies. Often, the businesses or their consultants create RFPs specifying the required site or building characteristics and the required or preferred community characteristics. Since searching through thousands of sites would be like looking for a needle in a haystack, companies commonly send the RFPs to state or regional economic development organizations and ask them to screen and submit any communities that meet the location criteria in the RFP. Sometimes companies forgo the RFP process and just informally spread the word that they are looking for a place to expand.

Smaller businesses, sometimes independently owned, often search for an expansion site in a more informal fashion. They may directly contact representatives from nearby cities and counties to ask about available sites and buildings, or they may search economic development or real estate websites for listings.

Regardless of the size or nature of the company, the process of matching buyer (the company) and seller (the community) is a two-way street. Companies actively look for expansion sites, and communities should also actively advertise their available sites and market themselves as a good business location. Communities can promote themselves and create market awareness in a number of ways including regular contacts with state or regional economic development organizations that receive RFPs, advertising in industry trade magazines and other business publications, or directly contacting businesses that might be in the expansion mode. The following box provides more information on community marketing and business recruiting.

2. *Business Retention and Expansion*

Just because a business is already located in a community does not mean that, if it needs to expand, it will do so in its current location. The need to expand could be driven by growth of an existing product, development of a new product, or any number of reasons that could prompt it to search for an additional location or even consider relocating the entire company. The expansion or relocation decisions of existing companies can be based on "push" factors making their current locations less attractive. For example, a company may grow dissatisfied with the local workforce, educational resources, or, as occurred in the previously mentioned examples of companies leaving California for Texas, the overall business climate including taxes and regulations.

Proactive communities can identify and work with existing companies and encourage them to expand where they are and not in other communities. Common business retention and expansion activities include:[11]

- *Identifying local companies that may be in the expansion mode or may be at a risk for relocation.* This can be done in many ways including monitoring local companies for production fluctuations, new product development announcements, or signs of potential merger or acquisition.
- *Working with local companies to help address any issues that may be driving them away from the community.* For example, a community could help a company meet its requirements for skilled labor and specialized training requirements through

---

[11] R. Pittman and T. Roberts. "Retaining and Expanding Existing Community Businesses." in R. Phillips, and R.H. Pittman. 2015. " *An Introduction To Community Development*, New York, N.Y: Routledge.

establishing internship programs in local high schools or
working in partnership with a local community college.

- *Building appreciation and loyalty among local businesses for the
  community* through, for example, industry appreciation ban-
  quets and newsletter articles.
- *Regular visits to local businesses* to identify issues and ways to
  address them. Economic development organizations frequently solicit volunteers to help with business retention and
  expansion efforts.

3. *New Business Startups*

Communities can encourage new business startups by providing assistance to them and becoming "entrepreneurial friendly."[12] New business
assistance programs can include:

- Low-cost shared space or "incubator" facilities for startup
  businesses that can include administrative support,
  meeting rooms, or even production facilities such as test
  kitchens.
- Training programs in business fundamentals such as strategic
  planning, accounting, and finance.
- Mentoring programs matching successful, experienced (often
  retired) business leaders with entrepreneurs.
- Information and research on important topics such as product
  market opportunities and competitor analysis.

New business startup assistance can be targeted to industries for which
a community has a comparative advantage. For example, Blue Ridge
Food Ventures in Asheville, North Carolina has a mission to "provide
infrastructure and technical assistance to enable small businesses entering
the marketplace with safe and wholesome foods and natural products,

---

[12] J. Gruidl and D. Markley. "Entrepreneurship as a Community Development
Strategy." in R. Phillips, and R.H. Pittman. 2015. *An Introduction To Community
Development*, New York, N.Y: Routledge.

thereby assisting in the creation of new businesses, new jobs, and new revenues for the region."[13]

Marketing Your Community: Your Brand, Your Audience, and Your Plan

Marketing your community is similar to marketing a business or a product. Your community might be a competitive location for business, a wonderful place to live, and a great place to visit, but even the best communities need marketing to achieve their goals and realize their vision. This reality is reflected in the large number of community and state marketing messages that appear every day through advertisements, e-mails, or other media.

Marketing is how you get your message and story into the world in a way that connects. It starts with keeping your audience top of mind and creating content that provides them with real value. **Branding** is defining who you are—the picture you are painting for your target markets of what your community holds for them.

Before you market your community, you need to know who you are as a community (clarify your brand) and who you are speaking to, and then create a plan to get the message out. Remember, your **brand** is more than a logo—it includes all points at which your audience connects with your community and the feelings it evokes. These can be displayed through your website, written materials, and more. Your brand also includes your current reputation and how people perceive your community.

Your audience includes different people so it helps to place them in different categories so you can understand exactly whom you are speaking to.

- Your **internal audience** is your community—people within your own office or organization, elected officials,

---

[13] "Blue Ridge Food Ventures—The Place Where Tasty Things Happen," 2021. *Blueridgefoodventures.Org*, https://blueridgefoodventures.org

and, really, all residents. You must get alignment with your internal audience so there is consistency with the message you are sending out about your community, as well as to build and sustain support for community and economic development efforts.

- Your **partners** will include any person or organization that can help and benefit from your community marketing efforts. For example, local real estate companies may be marketing the community to attract new commercial or residential buyers; their message should reflect the community brand. Certainly, all community and economic development organizations should adopt the brand. Sending out the same message through brand consistency across organizations can greatly enhance the power of marketing efforts.

- Your **external audience** includes those you want to attract to your community, such as new residents and businesses or organizations that will give the local economy a boost, bringing new jobs and growth.

For your marketing to achieve the results you want, you need to have a plan. You wouldn't start building a house without blueprints, so why try to market without a plan.

Your marketing plan should include the following elements:

- **Your Audience(s)**
- **Goals:** Goals bring clarity and help you focus your efforts so you're doing what will help achieve your desired results rather than wasting time on efforts that don't generate results. Don't set too many goals. Two to four is a good place to start.
- **Objectives:** What you use to measure your progress and success. Define what success looks like up front. Not everyone will have the same definition.
- **Strategy:** The approach you take to achieving your goals.

- **Tactics:** The action steps or marketing tools you use to achieve your goals and objectives. These can include e-mail marketing, social media, print or digital ads, public relations, and more.
- **Resources and Budget:** This includes your financial budget as well as your connections that can help you get the job done.
- **Schedule:** The final step in creating a marketing plan is developing a schedule of all the elements you want to include to map out what your plan will look like over time. A schedule:
  - Serves as a checks-and-balances system so you are creating a plan that is relevant to your organization and its stage of growth.
  - Allows you to be flexible when new opportunities come up or you realize something isn't working.

Marketing should be done with specific intention. Putting effort into branding your community and identifying the best target market groups is being intentional with your marketing efforts. It requires thinking about what you want people to do with the message you're putting out into the world. When you market with intention, your message is more likely to resonate with your audience than if you just shoot from the hip, post a couple of messages on social media, and hope it connects with people.

Community Enterprise: Expanding the Economic Development Stool

Now that we've introduced and explained the three-legged economic development stool, let's update this old model and metaphor. How? Let's add a fourth leg and convert our stool into a bench. A bench with four legs (Figure 4.4) is going to be more stable in the long run. So, what is this fourth leg? It's community enterprise. As we discussed in Chapter 3, community enterprise refers to actions by nonprofits, for-benefit private businesses, and the public/civic sector to develop entrepreneurial organizations. The focus of these enterprises also includes a community mission or benefit that will result from their activities. In some places, community enterprise, whether community supported or community owned, can be an important part of community prosperity.

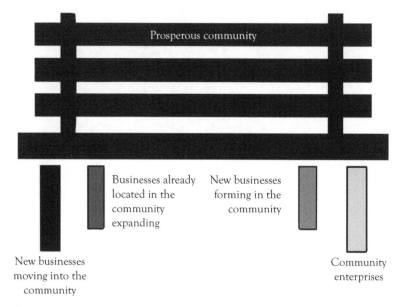

Prosperous community

Businesses already located in the community expanding

New businesses forming in the community

New businesses moving into the community

Community enterprises

Figure 4.4 The four-legged economic development bench

Actually, the other three legs of our economic development bench (the three legs of the original stool) can also be considered community enterprise. Communities provide many of the factors that established businesses and new business startups need, such as utilities, roads, education, and other public services. Communities often provide industrial and business parks where they can locate. In addition, communities sometimes offer tailored services, such as road or water and sewer line extensions, or labor training programs, as the part of an incentive package to win the site-selection competition over potentially hundreds of communities. In so many ways, successful economic development, and therefore community prosperity, results from a partnership between the private and public sectors. The private sector invests capital into the community, creating jobs, incomes and tax revenues, and the public sector supports that private investment by providing a prosperous-ready community. For some communities, the road to prosperity might be a little shorter and faster if they understood this partnership better.

Delivering Economic Development Services

In a course taught by the authors a few years ago, an elected official raised her hand and said, "Okay, I get it—the community development process helps build a prosperous-ready community and then economic development builds on that to help create a prosperous community; how can I best organize and fund economic development activities in my community?" The short answer was, "It depends on the situation"—a trite but true response because every community is unique. Here are some guidelines to help answer this question:

- **Economic development activities should be tailored to the specific needs of a community.** A mountain town away from a major highway with a tourism-based economy might want to emphasize small business development oriented toward the hospitality and retail sectors rather than business recruitment. However, promoting the community as a great location for small technology-based professional firms that can deliver their services remotely, or something similar, might be a good strategy for economic diversification. Contrastingly, a larger town with good highway and rail service and lots of developable land might want to concentrate its economic development efforts on recruiting advanced manufacturing companies or distribution centers.
- **The organization and funding of economic development activities depend on the political landscape of a community.** There are almost as many models for structuring and delivering economic development activities or services as there are individual communities. These models range from mainly public sector delivery and funding to mainly private sector delivery and funding and variations in between:

- Public Sector Model: Economic development activities publicly funded, usually within an office of economic development in county or city government.
- Private Sector Model: Economic development activities within a private nonprofit organization.
- Public/Private Model: Economic development activities within a private nonprofit organization jointly supported and funded by the public and private sectors.

A community's political situation often influences the type of economic development model chosen. For example, in communities without a strong history of cooperation among local governments, it can be more difficult to form a jointly funded public/private partnership.

In communities that can support them, public/private models can offer significant advantages. Typically, they are structured as private, nonprofit organizations with funding from both local governments and private sector contributions or membership dues. The boards of directors of these organizations include representatives from local governments, key community organizations, and the business sector. They often are Internal Revenue Service certified 501(c)(3) charitable organizations supporting tax-deductible contributions or 501(c)(6) membership organizations eligible to receive proceeds from certain local taxes.

Partnerships between the public sector and private sector for economic development can offer numerous advantages. Sometimes public funding and support for economic development can suddenly change when a new administration comes into office. Public/private organizations with diversified funding can provide more continuity and consistency to economic development activities. In addition, public/private economic development organizations with broad-based board representation can serve as a platform for increased cooperation, communication, and trust among local governments and private sector businesses and organizations. This can significantly improve the community development process, helping the community reach a consensus on a number of issues and create a unified vision for the future.

Regional Partnerships

A growing trend in economic development is regional partnerships among cities and counties. Local economies are naturally regional—workers commuting over city and county lines, businesses buying inputs and services from and selling to other businesses in a region, and consumers patronizing retail shops and restaurants within a region. In addition, greater marketing reach can be obtained by combining the resources of multiple cities and counties in a region. For example, while an economic development organization for an individual county might not have a sufficient budget to attend a national or international industry trade show, a regional economic development marketing organization could represent all of the economic development organizations in a region. If, as a result, a new company moves into the region, all cities and counties are likely to benefit as workers and shoppers travel within the region. For example, the Upstate South Carolina Alliance (Figure 4.5) represents the cities and counties in the Greenville/Spartanburg combined metro area. The

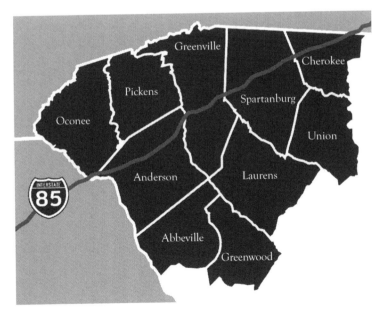

Figure 4.5 Upstate South Carolina Alliance

Source: www.upstatescalliance.com/site-selection/map-center/

Alliance markets the multi county area as a place where companies can choose to locate in an urban, suburban, or rural location, and still enjoy the benefits of the entire upstate area including its labor force and transportation infrastructure.

Bringing It All Together: Community Economic Development and Prosperity

Throughout the book we have defined community development and economic development as processes and outcomes. Chapter 3 showed how the process of community development, including creating a vision and addressing community issues through an inclusive strategy, paves the way to the outcome of a prosperous-ready community. This chapter described how the process of economic development builds on that foundation, increasing the flow of money into the community and creating new jobs and higher incomes leading to an economically prosperous community. Chapter 2 provided the groundwork for all of this by offering a new, more comprehensive definition of community prosperity composed of four components: basic needs, quality of life, social needs, and the economy. Using the roadmap to prosperity as an illustration, Chapter 2 showed that the four components are highly interrelated, with a strong local economy providing a foundation for the other three components.

These links are shown in Figure 4.6: The Community Economic Development Prosperity Chain. The process works as follows:

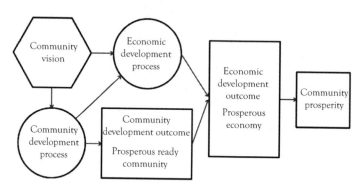

Figure 4.6 The community and economic development prosperity chain

- The chain begins with a **community vision**. Just as a vision or mission statement for a company or organization helps guide its actions and policies, a vision for a community helps unite residents behind common goals.
- The vision helps guide the **community development process**, leading to the outcome of a prosperous-ready community attractive to businesses and residents. A prosperous-ready community also provides three of the prosperous community components: basic needs, quality-of-life enhancements, and social needs. These then feed through the flow to the outcome of community prosperity.
- The community vision also helps guide the **economic development process**, including its funding, organizational structure, and programs.
- Finally, the outcome of community development (a prosperous-ready community) and the economic development process combine to produce a **prosperous economy** and finally our end goal: a balanced, **prosperous community**.

Figure 4.6 illustrates a key point of the book that is worth repeating: economic development success and prosperity depend heavily on building a prosperous-ready community through the community development process. Unfortunately, many communities miss or ignore this point and handicap their ability to achieve success. As discussed in this chapter, a community with a good workforce, infrastructure, and other factors that businesses look for and that offers a good quality of life that residents want is primed for success. "Fatal flaws," such as limited water and sewer service or a poor school system, can greatly handicap economic development efforts and community prosperity. No community is perfect, and all communities have relative strengths and weaknesses. Targeting economic development efforts with this in mind is a smart policy.

In theory and practice, community development and economic development are inextricably linked, and many experts and practitioners in the field prefer a more encompassing term. The authors of one article use the term "community economic development" which has "a broader dimension that includes public capital, technology and innovation, society and culture, institutions, and the decision making capacity of the community."[14] Does it sound familiar? As we advocate in the book, community economic development is the key to building prosperous communities.

Prosperous Community Toolbox

Read, Reflect, Share, and Act

The theme of Chapter 4 is building on the foundation of a prosperous-ready community with the economic development process to achieve the outcome of a prosperous community. It starts with a simple model of how money flows into and out of your community to create wealth. However, true community prosperity goes much deeper—it also involves defining economic development for your community and proactive marketing to achieve your vision of prosperity. The Chapter 4 tools are intended to help you assess how your community has grown and changed in recent years; it's competitive advantages; your community's economic development process; and collaboration with surrounding communities for regional economic development programs and opportunities.

4.1 Assess the growth and change that has occurred in your community over the past 5 to 10 years. Using the boxes "How Does Your Local Economy Measure Up?" from Chapter 2 and "Is It Economic Development or Just Growth?" from this chapter as guides, decide whether your community has experienced economic development or just growth. Are income levels in your community increasing? Is your workforce becoming more skilled? Is recent growth consistent with

---

[14] R. Shaffer, S. Deller, and D. Marcouiller. 2006. "Rethinking Community Economic Development," *Economic Development Quarterly* 20, No. 1, p. 64.

your community's vision for the future? Use the results of this assessment as a call to action and, if necessary, a course correction in your community's roadmap to prosperity.

4.2 Assess your community as a competitive location for businesses and other job-generating organizations. Through focus groups, individual interviews, and surveys, obtain broad input from existing businesses and organizations on the strengths and weaknesses of your community as a business location. Statistical benchmarking of your community to others in terms of wage rates, cost of living, and other key locational factors is also extremely useful. Some communities engage consultants to help them with this process and compare them to other communities. An outside, objective viewpoint is often the best way to evaluate your community. Develop plans to address the weaknesses and build on the strengths.

4.3. Evaluate the economic development process in your community. What organizations in your community directly deliver economic development services or are otherwise involved? Understand how these organizations are funded and staffed. Are they delivering the kinds of economic development services such as marketing, business recruitment, business retention, and new business startup assistance discussed in this chapter as appropriate for your community? Compare the economic development process in your community with other communities. State departments of economic development or outside consultants can assist in this comparison.

4.4 Determine the status and/or potential for regional economic development programs and activities. Does your community currently cooperate with surrounding communities or counties to promote your region to companies, tourists, or other appropriate target markets? How successful have those efforts been and how can your community promote more regional cooperation for economic development?

Visit www.prosperousplaces.org/rebooteconomics_toolbox/ to download templates and resources for the Chapter 4 tools.

If you skipped the chapter and came directly here to see what Osceola, Arkansas did to reboot its economy, we understand. We invite you now to read the chapter to see the bigger picture and overall process they followed. To those of you who have read the chapter, congratulations; the rest of the story will be more meaningful.

Osceola, Arkansas—The Rest of the Story

Let's review the question posed at the beginning of the chapter: how did Osceola, Arkansas (Figure 4.7) reboot itself from "almost the point of no return" to a healthy community with thousands of new jobs and billions of dollars in new corporate investment? The answer in a nutshell: by understanding and following the principles of good community and economic development as described in the book. Osceola is an excellent example of how to lay a foundation for success with community development and then build on it with economic development.

The first step in Osceola's recovery was to create a more prosperous-ready community attractive to businesses. With Osceola's troubled public schools, local businesses were having difficulty finding labor with the necessary skill sets, so they began to work with the city administration to find a solution. The community decided to ask the state for permission to establish a charter school that could produce educated students with good work skills. After several community meetings and differences of opinion, the community united behind the effort and opened a charter school.

Figure 4.7 Osceola, AR

Encouraged by their success with the charter school, Osceola reached out to the Arkansas Economic Development Commission and statewide utilities and told them it wanted to pursue new business investment aggressively and was willing to invest public money into the right projects. Through these outreach contacts, Osceola discovered that Denso, a Japanese-owned auto parts company, was looking for a manufacturing site in the southern states. City representatives showed Denso the charter school and explained how the community had come together to address its education and labor problem. Denso decided to locate the plant in Osceola, creating 400 jobs. While Denso executives cited the improved labor force as a reason for selecting Osceola, they also were impressed with how the community came together and solved one of its biggest problems. An executive from Denso was quoted in *The Wall Street Journal* as saying, "It was their aggressiveness that really impressed us."

Despite Osceola's educational reform and workforce improvement, Denso initially still had questions about Osceola's commitment to continuous improvement in the schools when making the location decision. On this concern, the Denso executive was quoted as saying, "Is there a future here? Are they doing things that are going to drive them forward? Do they have that commitment to do it? We saw that continuously in Osceola." Denso decided to locate in Osceola not only because of the city's past achievements, but also because they were convinced the city would continue to practice good community development principles and move forward. Osceola's success story was featured on the front page of the national edition of *The Wall Street Journal* in 2006.

The story continues after the Denso win. Voters in the city passed a one-half cent sales tax to provide continuing support for economic development activities, including workforce training and incentives. Some of the sales tax money was earmarked to help support the newly formed Great River Economic Development Foundation, a public-private partnership among Mississippi County, Osceola, and Blytheville, the county's largest town. Building on an emerging cluster of metals product companies already in the area, the Foundation, county, and the cities together were able to attract new companies to the area including the previously mentioned Big River Steel Company with its initial investment of $1.3 billion.

Over the past 20 years, according to the Great River Economic Development Foundation, 4,100 new jobs have been created in Mississippi County, along with private capital investment of approximately $4 billion. The annual payroll from these new jobs is approximately $130 million. The total economic impact of the new jobs, payrolls, and investment is even larger than these numbers when the multiplier or re-spending effect is taken into account. Total public investment in these projects over 20 years through grants, worker training, and other incentives has been approximately $42 million, a sound return by most any measure (recall our discussion that community enterprise is a term that can apply broadly to economic development, even if the investment came from the private sector). The story of Osceola, Blytheville, and Mississippi County is an encouraging example of good teamwork, and illustrates several key factors leading to economic development success that we have discussed in this chapter:

- Community development lays the foundation for economic development. What originally attracted Denso was Osceola's proven success in turning one of its biggest liabilities, education, into one of its biggest strengths. Along with Osceola's commitment of continuing support, that success convinced Denso that the city could accommodate its future needs.

- Osceola had a proactive approach to economic development and stepped up its commitment to recruit new industries and spread the word.
- Cooperation among local governments with more resources in the same county and beyond (regional partnerships) can facilitate greater economic development success.
- Understanding and marketing on local strengths, in this case, an emerging cluster of metals companies in the area, can contribute to economic development success. This is one way the "target industry" approach can make economic development programs more effective and efficient.
- Community and economic development efforts should be ongoing, not just one-time events. Countywide public and private efforts spearheaded by the Great River Economic Development Foundation continued after the Denso success. Together, Osceola and Mississippi County were able to recover from the economic shock of the Fruit of the Loom plant closing and, later, the gradual reduction in employment of another larger company in town, American Greetings.

CHAPTER 5

Sustaining Prosperity

We began this book by welcoming you on the journey to community prosperity and noting how much the communities we live in affect our everyday life and even define us. We took the first steps of our journey with a question and a promise. The question was why some communities thrive and grow while others stagnate or decline, and why some communities are able to face adversity and reboot while others cannot. We asked, metaphorically, if there was a secret sauce or fairy dust for community success. We still haven't found any fairy dust, but we do hope the book has provided you with a recipe for the sauce. But, please don't keep it secret like a treasured family recipe—share it with others to help them achieve prosperity. Remember our mantra of Read, Reflect, Share, and Act.

We noted in the Introduction that now is a good time for this book, ironically due in part to the pandemic during which people in towns and cities everywhere learned to work together better to address a common problem facing their communities and the world. And, just like the COVID-19 vaccine, we expressed our hope that learning how to build a prosperous community would provide a degree of protection from future shocks and contribute to sustainable prosperity for your community.

Our promise was to provide you with a toolbox for community prosperity, and we hope we have lived up to that, not only through the tools at the end of each chapter and the associated worksheets at ProsperousPlaces.org, but also by providing you with the knowledge of how to use them. Even the best toolbox will not make a carpenter out of someone who doesn't know how to use what's inside. Let's reflect now on our journey and see how far we've come and how much knowledge we've gained.

New Normal for Your Community

As we recovered from the initial pandemic, we kept our fingers crossed, hoping, first, that any additional rounds of infection from variants of the COVID-19 virus would not be as serious, and, second, that we would be better prepared to deal with them. The COVID-19 "echo" round with the Delta and other variants has challenged the first hope, but the knowledge gained through research and experience with the initial pandemic has provided us with tools (including vaccines) to cope better with current and future infections.

In some parts of the world, the COVID-19 virus is still out of control and variants are spreading. Data presented in Chapter 1 show clearly that the economic impact of the COVID-19 pandemic was severe—a multigenerational event in some ways comparable to the Great Depression. The real focus of Chapter 1, however, was whether the pandemic has created a "new normal" with lasting social and economic effects. We noted in Chapter 1 that the term new normal has been frequently used and sometimes applied to events that had little, if any, lasting effect. The question then becomes are we crying wolf if we call life after the pandemic a new normal?

Data and information presented in Chapter 1 make the case that we are not. Chapter 1 cites expert opinion, studies, and surveys on the long-term effects of the pandemic stemming from business closures, quarantines, and the new remote "geography of work." The evidence is compelling that remote work will continue to be a preferred practice for many companies and employees. This means that remote work employees are freer to reside where they prefer and not necessarily close to their employer, and companies may not necessarily be tied to locations where workers live. The new geography of work offers challenges and opportunities—challenges for some urban cores that may lose workers and companies but also opportunities for suburban and rural communities to attract them.

The pandemic struck hard and fast, sparing very few communities from an economic and social shock unequaled for decades. The pandemic gave virtually all cities and towns a taste of what can happen to communities at any time due to the loss of a major employer or other economic shock. If there is even a hint of a silver lining in some corner of the COVID-19 storm clouds, it could be that many communities have learned a bit more about residents working together to address immediate challenges, how to meet future challenges, and how to find opportunities in the postpandemic new normal.

How hard was your community hit by the pandemic and what do you think will be the lasting effects? Do you believe there are opportunities for your community in the postpandemic new normal and new geography of work? We urge you to use the tools in the Chapter 1 toolbox to consider these questions.

Prosperity Revisited

We hope the book has helped you develop a better understanding and appreciation for your community. How prosperous do you now think your community is within the framework of the four prosperous community components? A key point of Chapter 2 is that the first step in building a prosperous community is to define what you are building. Just as you should not build a house without a blueprint, you should not try to build a community without a plan and vision. We began Chapter 2 by noting that there are many different definitions of individual prosperity — some emphasize wealth and financial success while others emphasize a "rich and full life." That led us to consider the definition of community prosperity by examining two contrasting communities, Riverside and Port City.

The question of which town is more prosperous then led us to consider studies and surveys about factors that residents prefer in their communities. Physical factors such as safety and parks and recreation were highly rated as were social factors including a feeling of shared community and opportunities for involvement and service. Economic factors such as the availability of good paying jobs were also listed but were ranked behind some of the physical and social factors. We noted that these preferences for community factors closely reflect Maslow's hierarchy of needs pyramid with basic needs such as food, shelter, and safety at the base supporting higher-order needs corresponding to community involvement and a sense of belonging.

Based on this discussion, we identified four components that define community prosperity: basic needs, quality of life, social needs, and economy. We then listed some specific community factors or characteristics that fall under each prosperous community component. For example, safety and education were listed under the basic needs component and a strong employment base and economic opportunity for all residents were listed under the economy component.

A discussion of the strong interactions among the four components led us to conceptualize a roadmap to community prosperity. We noted that each community should customize and prioritize the factors under each of the four community components that are most important to them—the beginning of a custom community blueprint. We drew a ring road around the four prosperous community components connecting them to symbolize the synergies and interactions among them. At the heart of the roadmap was the vision a community has for its future that is critical to customizing and prioritizing the important community factors and understanding the interactions among them.

We concluded Chapter 2 with the observation that just as a well-run company should make investment decisions based on how they contribute to its mission and profitability, a community should make strategic and budget decisions based on how they contribute to its vision and definition of prosperity. To illustrate this, we introduced a third town to join Riverside and Port City in a Tale of Three Cities. Overton was based on the real-life story of Tupelo and Lee County, Mississippi that achieved sustainable prosperity by building and following their own roadmap. As we conclude our journey, we would like to introduce you to another community with an inspiring story that has also followed the roadmap to achieve prosperity—Fairfield, Iowa. Tupelo and Fairfield used the tools we discuss in this book to create a vision and customized roadmap to prosperity. If your community hasn't done this already, we urge you to get started!

"Silicorn" Valley

Fairfield, IA

Figure 5.1 "Silicorn" valley

Imagine a growing, diverse city with a strong economy including traditional manufacturing companies, high-tech startups, solar energy
projects, and financial management firms. Add to this a strong arts
community and an international school of "consciousness-based education" that turns out hundreds of computer science majors. This
thriving city must be located on the west coast or east coast, right? Actually, Fairfield is a town located among the cornfields and hog farms
of Southeast Iowa's Jefferson County with a regional population under
20,000 people. The Mayor of Fairfield, the place dubbed "America's
most unusual town" by Oprah Winfrey, attributes the community's
success to a great quality of life culture and entrepreneurial culture.

The rebooting process in Fairfield started many years ago when
Maharishi University of Management relocated there from Santa Barbara,
California to buildings vacated by a local college. Today, the city's

sense of community and support for businesses encourages people who move there to "figure out how to stay," says a spokesman for Sky Factory, a company founded there in 2002 that produces decorative ceiling tile. Other successful companies in Fairfield include Creative Edge that makes flooring for large institutions, Bovard Studios that makes and restores stained glass windows, and Cambridge Investment Research that boasts 700 employees and over $70 billion in assets under management.

Fairfield is a fine example of a community following the roadmap to prosperity. According to the Iowa Economic Development Authority:

- Fairfield works in partnership with public and private entities. Additionally, rather than trying to imitate other communities, Fairfield embraces its uniqueness and pursues an economic and community development vision that is best suited for the diversity of business and culture that fits best there.
- Prosperity in Fairfield and Jefferson County is the result of planning, not serendipity. The Fairfield Economic Development Association has six strategic priorities:
  o Community development
  o New business and industry
  o Existing business and industry
  o Internal and external marketing
  o Education
  o Workforce development

In Fairfield, the prosperous community components reinforce each other: a strong economy supports a good quality of life including arts (e.g., the Sondheim Center for the Performing Arts) and a mix of international restaurants (more per capita than San Francisco). These community factors, in turn, encourage entrepreneurs and business owners to stay and grow their companies. Residents are proud of Fairfield's success and engagement in the community.

Sources:
2021. *Desmoinesregister.Com,* www.desmoinesregister.com/story/money/business/2016/05/31/why-iowa-town-thriving-when-so-many-arent/83973154/
  Submission to the authors by the Iowa Economic Development Authority.

Laying the Foundation

In Chapter 3 we discussed using the process of community development to create a prosperous-ready community that is appealing to business and residents alike, thus creating a solid foundation for the process and outcome of economic development including more and better jobs, and higher incomes. We saw that community development is about connecting people and resources and building on the "capitals" that all communities have.

During the pandemic people who were working and schooling at home were apparently also exercising more. Health and fitness equipment revenue more than doubled from March to October in 2020, and sales of treadmills increased 135 percent.[1] All that conditioning undoubtedly helped build healthier bodies more capable of engaging in regular activities such as cutting the grass or playing a game of pickup basketball. And, as many of us know from experience, after the first couple of workouts, we are in better condition for the next ones. As we discussed in Chapter 3, the same holds true for community development. By engaging in the process of community development, improving social cohesion, and building human and social capital, communities become better conditioned to do more of it and become better at it.

All these elements or community capitals are ingredients for the recipe to create community prosperity. Sometimes, we see places changing

---

[1] "The Pandemic's Home-Workout Revolution May Be Here To Stay," 2021. *The Washington Post,* www.washingtonpost.com/road-to-recovery/2021/01/07/home-fitness-boom/

due to the actions of just one person or one institution, but community development is a group activity with strategies emerging from the collective decision of many people to take action. Strategies for community improvement are driven by vision and require communitywide initiatives and collaboration to succeed. It is helpful to think of community development as *community building*, including building the components for a prosperous-ready community.

The Final Step to a Prosperous Community

Chapters 1 through 3 set the stage for the final step toward prosperity outlined in Chapter 4—the process and outcome of economic development. The first steps are to develop a vision and strategic plan and start building a prosperous-ready community. This will make economic development efforts more successful and help create the kind of prosperity the community wants to achieve. Without laying the foundation, a lot of time and money can be wasted with little result except increased frustration and doubts about a community's ability to improve.

Chapter 4 began with the inspiring story of Osceola, Arkansas that did so many things right. They created a prosperous-ready community and then engaged successfully in the process of economic development, specifically engaging in a marketing outreach program that led to a tremendous economic development outcome—billions of dollars of business investment and thousands of new jobs for the community and region. As we saw in Chapter 2's wealth and cash flow "tank" diagram, these billions of dollars circulate and recirculate within the community to create even more wealth and jobs. The wealth tank diagram clearly shows the simple but sometimes overlooked concept that increasing the flow of money into the local economy and decreasing the outflow will help create community prosperity.

Next in Chapter 4, we discussed ways to increase the inflow of money from business investment, noting that businesses naturally want to locate in communities that have an available and productive workforce, good transportation services, and other key factors of production to stay competitive and earn a profit. In addition, business owners and managers also prefer communities with quality-of-life enhancements, a good education system, and opportunities for community involvement—in other words, communities that rate well in all four prosperous community components. Achieving that involves the process of community development.

Just as successful businesses concentrate on their core product and customer markets, a community should do the same and not try to be "all things to all people." Success in marketing comes from targeting those sectors and industries for which the community has a comparative advantage—a community with a college engineering program recruiting tech companies or a community with good weather and health care recruiting retirees and vacationers.

However, encouraging new investment into a community (increasing the inflow and raising the community wealth level) is just one leg of the traditional economic development stool. The two other legs, working to help ensure that existing local businesses stay and expand in the community instead of relocating—often referred to as business retention and expansion—and supporting entrepreneurs and startup businesses are just as important, or more so, than recruiting new businesses. However, a new business moving to town often garners front page headlines while the expansion of an existing company or the launch of a new one are often taken for granted. The city of Fairfield, Iowa, profiled earlier is an example of a community that understands the three legs of the economic development stool and includes the care of existing businesses and nurture of new businesses in its vision and strategic plan.

The growth of community enterprises led us in Chapter 4 to suggest a new metaphor for economic prosperity: a four-legged bench instead of a three-legged stool. Community enterprises take a variety of forms, including employee-owned businesses or businesses owned by local public investors. For example, they can be found in rural towns to provide services that privately owned businesses are not supplying such as a grocery store, or in urban areas where "big box" stores have crowded out smaller specialty stores. We concluded that discussion with the observation that to some extent, all businesses are community enterprises. Business prosperity and community prosperity are intertwined—communities provide services such as roads and education to support businesses and, in turn, businesses support the community by creating jobs, incomes, and tax revenues.

To successfully engage in the economic development process and deliver these services, a community must devote adequate resources to the effort (including staff and funding), and Chapter 4 provides some guidelines on this. Some communities look at economic development funding as just another budget cost item. However, economic development efforts can, and often do, return to the community much more money than they cost by helping create new jobs and higher incomes. Money spent on the economic development process should be viewed as an investment, not just a cost, and the returns it generates should be monitored and evaluated.

Sustaining a Prosperous Community

Detroit, Michigan was once an economic and cultural powerhouse. For decades after World War II, the "Big Three" in Detroit dominated U.S. automobile production, creating a healthy middle class composed of white- and blue-collar workers. This prosperity helped make Detroit a center of arts and culture, giving birth to the "Motown" sound that still gets fingers snapping and toes tapping to this day. Detroit is now a shell of its former self with urban decay and a population 60 percent less than at its peak in the 1950s. However, like green shoots after a forest fire, signs of rebirth are occurring as entrepreneurs and urban pioneers start new companies and rebuild grand homes in a low cost of living environment. Detroit is a long way from rebooting, but perhaps these early signs bode well for the future of the city.

In contrast, Tupelo, Mississippi, featured in Chapter 2, has rebooted its economy twice from agriculture to manufacturing and then to advanced manufacturing, keeping up with changing conditions and sustaining prosperity. Atlanta, Georgia transformed itself from the capital of the "Old South" to the capital of the "New South" by first becoming a transportation hub and then attracting global companies and millions of new residents by providing a good low-cost business climate and high quality of life with affordable housing and world-class universities. While Detroit struggled to adapt to the "new normal" of its declining auto industry, the small city of Tupelo and the large metropolis of Atlanta not only adapted to the new normal of global markets, supply chains, transportation, and logistics, but they also anticipated these developments.

Once a community comes up on the "plane" of community prosperity like a boat getting up to speed, it must keep its hand on the throttle and continue to supply the fuel required to support prosperity in the form of community and economic development processes and outcomes. We urge you to keep your community's roadmap to prosperity with you at all times and update it as external or internal conditions change.

We have greatly enjoyed our journey with you along the road to prosperity and our time together in community "reboot" camp. We look forward to further travels and adventures together.

Resources and References

Selected publications by the authors:

Phillips, R., and R. Pittman. n.d. "An Introduction to Community Development."
www.routledge.com/An-Introduction-to-Community-Development/
Phillips-Pittman/p/book/9780415703550?gclid=CjwKCAjwgISIBhBfEi
wALE19STY6ZJcFJ41CDBDK0_EuSjvCjD9KuD9j9xeRA92aJHiZqY8Qi
s3EhRoCBO8QAvD_BwE

Phillips, R., M. Brennan, and T. Li. n.d. "Culture, Community, and Development."
www.amazon.com/Culture-Community-Development-Research-
Practice/dp/1138593966/ref=sr_1_3?dchild=1&qid=1627395227
&refinements=p_27%3ARhonda+Phillips&s=books&sr=1-3

Phillips, R., E. Antczak, and B. Seifer. 2013. *Sustainable Communities.*
Hoboken: Taylor and Francis. www.amazon.com/Sustainable-Communities-
Creating-Earthscan-Community-ebook/dp/B00EKN8TI8/ref=sr_1_6?
dchild=1&qid=1627395227&refinements=p_27%3ARhonda+Phillips&s=
books&sr=1-6

Phillips, R., and C. Wong. n.d. "Handbook of Community Well-being
Research." www.amazon.com/Handbook-Community-Well-Being-International-
Handbooks-ebook/dp/B01N4DG8VP/ref=sr_1_21?dchild=1&qid
=1627395455&refinements=p_27%3ARhonda+Phillips&s=books&sr=1-21

Other Resources:

DeFilippis, J., and S. Saegert. 2012. *The Community Development Reader.* New
York, N.Y: Routledge. www.amazon.com/Community-Development-
Reader-2nd/dp/0415507766/ref=sr_1_5?dchild=1&keywords=communit
y+development&qid=1627395621&sr=8-5#:~:text=The%20Community-
,Development,-Reader%2C%202nd%20Edition%202nd

Gordon, G. 2021. *Understanding Community Economic Growth Decline.* [S.l.]:
Routledge. www.amazon.com/Understanding-Community-Economic-Growth-
Decline/dp/103209530X/ref=sr_1_8?dchild=1&keywords=Communi-
ty+Economic+Development&qid=1627396107&s=books&sr=1-8#:~:-
text=Understanding%20Community%20Economic-,Growth,-and%20
Decline%201st

Green, G., and A. Haines. n.d. *Asset Building & Community Development.*
www.amazon.com/Asset-Building-Community-Development-Green/

dp/1483344037/ref=sr_1_9?dchild=1&keywords=Community+Economi
c+Development&qid=1627396107&s=books&sr=1-9#:~:text=Asset%20
Building%20%26-,Community,-Development%20Fourth%20Edition
Ratner, S. n.d. *Wealth Creation.* www.amazon.com/Wealth-Creation-Shanna-
Ratner/dp/0367257424/ref=sr_1_10?dchild=1&keywords=Communi-
ty+Economic+Development&qid=1627396107&s=books&sr=1-10#:~:tex-
t=Creation%3A%20A%20New-,Framework,-for%20Rural%20Economic
Gruber, J. 2020. *Building Community: Twelve Principles for a Healthy Future,*
1st ed. New Society Publishers. www.amazon.com/Building-Community-
Twelve-Principles-Healthy-ebook/dp/B07V5RD4MJ/ref=sr_1_13?dchild=1
&keywords=Community+Economic+Development&qid=1627396107&s=
books&sr=1-13#:~:text=%2B%20Follow-,Building,-Community%3A%20
Twelve%20Principles
University of Minnesota Extension. 2021. Understanding Local Economies.
[online] Available at https://extension.umn.edu/economic-development/
understanding-local-economies (accessed July 28, 2021).

Journals:

"Community Development." *Journal of the Community Development Society.*
[online] Available at www.comm-dev.org/professional-development/cds-
journal (accessed July 28, 2021).
Lyons, T., and R. Hamlin. 2001. *Creating an Economic Development Action
Plan.* Westport, Conn.: Praeger. www.amazon.com/Creating-Economic-
Development-Action-Plan/dp/027596809X#:~:text=an%20Economic%20
Development-,Action,-Plan%3A%20A%20Guide
"Local Development & Society." *Journal of the Community Development
Society.* [online] Available at www.tandfonline.com/doi/abs/10.1080/1557
5330902918956 (accessed July 28, 2021).

About the Authors

For over three decades, **Robert Pittman** has been a thought leader and innovator in community and economic development. He has held senior management positions in the industry including Director of Economic Development Consulting for a global engineering and consulting firm. He has helped communities, regions and states develop and implement community and economic development strategies, and worked with companies to find the best locations for their operations. He has also served as a university professor teaching graduate courses in community and economic development, and authored numerous articles and books in the field. He holds degrees in economics from Emory and Northwestern universities.

Committed to helping build communities via her collaborative leadership approaches, **Rhonda Phillips** enjoys working across the globe, presenting at the OECD and many other events. Rhonda was recently appointed as an International Core Faculty Member for youth and community development with UNESCO and recognized with the International Society of Quality-of-Life Studies annual conference Rhonda G. Phillips Endowed Track for the Promotion of Community Development and Community Well-Being. Rhonda is the first woman to graduate with a doctorate in city and regional planning from the Georgia Institute of Technology.

Amanda Sutt grew up in the branding and marketing industry. Her mother founded Rock Paper Scissors in 1986 and Amanda officially joined the business as a project manager after graduating from Appalachian State University. Amanda assumed the role of CEO and Creative Director, leading her team to support clients in a number of industries, including community and economic development, franchises, and nonprofits and other service providers. Amanda was also a certified EMyth Business Coach, which allows her to support marketing clients by helping build internal systems to streamline marketing operations and accelerating results in an increasingly complex marketing climate.

Index

Made in the USA
Columbia, SC
24 July 2022

63932410R00091